C000064625

AT THE END OF THE DAY

PAUL BYRNES

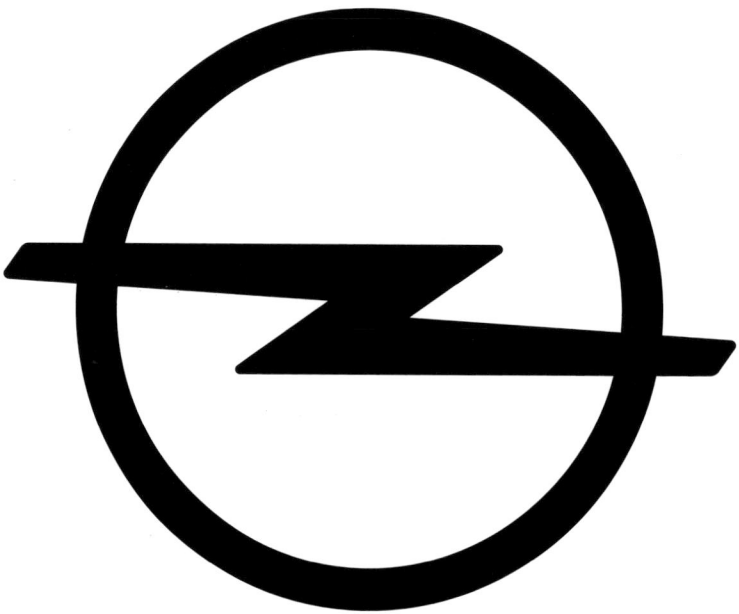

Ireland's No.1 Supporter

Opel has been woven into the tapestry of the Irish motoring landscape history for over fifty years. The foundations were laid in the 1960s with two plants in Dublin and Cork assembling both the Opel Rekord, and family favourite Opel Kadett. Still today, most Irish households can recall fond memories of the family Opel of their childhood, which continues to shape their choice of Opel for their motoring needs today. Often these memories can be linked with some of the greatest sporting moments in Irish history, as both Opel and Sport have been inextricably linked in Ireland for over 30 years.

From 'Big Jack' and the 'Boys in Green', adventures at the Euros in '88, Italia '90 and USA '94, the iconic Opel Jersey, is still found in the drawers of true supporters and authentic footballing hipsters around the country.

By 2006, Gaelic Games took centre-stage as Opel went on to sponsor Ireland's indigenous pastime as the Official Car Partner of the GAA. From supporting Ireland's talent at grass-roots with the Opel Kit for Clubs programme, through to celebrating the best-of-the-best as proud sponsors of the GAA GPA Opel All-Stars, Opel has supported this country's talent across all levels.

Many of the sporting legends, who have delivered the iconic sporting moments in history, have their own fond memories of the role the "family Opel" played in their travels through their sporting development. Some of the legends featured in this book have and indeed currently represent Opel as brand ambassadors.

As they take a bow off the sporting stage, this book gives a unique insight into 14 of Ireland's biggest sporting stars from various disciplines, on how they have moved into a new phase of excellence, 'At The End of the Day', as they face into the next stage of their lives after the final whistle.

One thing is for sure - they have all inspired others in their sporting and personal journeys.

Opel are proud to support Paul Byrnes as sponsor of 'At The End Of The Day'. This book will be a treasured possession on coffee tables around the country, hailing the great legends of Irish sport who have changed the face of a nation over the years.

Enjoy the read,
Dave Sheeran

At the End of the Day
By Paul Byrnes
ISBN: 978-1-911180-74-6
Copyright©2017 Paul Byrnes
ALL RIGHTS RESERVED.
International copyright secured.

Published in Ireland by Lettertec.

lettertec

Dedicated to my father Tommy

who loved sport just as much as I do today.

CONTENTS

BACKGROUND

Close your eyes.

Imagine preparing for the biggest game of your life. Imagine the blood, sweat and tears that go into such. Imagine the dressing room beforehand. Imagine playing with the best against the best. Imagine the roar of the crowd. Imagine winning. It must be the greatest feeling in the world.

Now imagine stepping off the stage. You're no longer a player, you're now a former player. The days of competing are over. You're leaving something you loved behind and you don't want it to end. Kerry football legend Colm 'Gooch' Cooper retired in 2017 after a truly remarkable career. "I'd love to play for Kerry for the rest of my life" he said, "but time catches up with everyone." A lot of sportspeople struggle with retirement and in many cases it can be difficult to move on. You go from 80,000 people screaming your name to total silence. There's no longer any structure in your life. There's no one telling you what to do and when to do it. It can be a very strange feeling. You've put your life on hold for years and suddenly it's all over. Athletes are incredibly driven people. They love winning and they hate losing. They know that nothing ever replaces the intensity of training, that buzz of playing or that winning feeling. Once they retire they start asking questions and looking for answers. Just what do I do now? Is that really it? Who am I? Did I retire too early or was I pushed?

One of the greatest hurlers of all time, Kilkenny's Henry Shefflin retired in 2015. "In my opinion, there are two types of people who retire. Those that want to and those that don't. I wanted to."

After winning a record 10 All Ireland senior hurling medals and 11 All Star awards, King Henry announced he was retiring from the inter-county scene shortly after Ballyhale beat Kilmallock in the All Ireland club final at Croke Park. It was an incredible end to an incredible career.

Twelve months earlier another legend of Irish sport, Brian O'Driscoll retired from the game.

In his last international game, the final day of the RBS 6 Nations, Ireland beat France in Paris for only the second time in 42 years to win the championship. It was a fitting end to a truly wonderful career. A week earlier, O'Driscoll produced a man of the match performance against Italy before the Aviva said goodbye to a superstar.

Both O'Driscoll and Shefflin have gone on to enjoy very successful careers in the media. But not every player gets such opportunities. Not every player finishes his or her career in such glorious fashion. You get injured—just ask Paul O'Connell—you get dropped or your body just says NO.

In this book, 14 Irish sporting greats talk about life after sport, filling the void and moving on. They also describe their most memorable moments and their darkest days. They are all truly remarkable people.

AP McCoy is 20 times champion jockey. He rode his first winner in 1992 at seventeen years of age. He's a machine and we're unlikely to ever see the likes of him again.

Tipperary's Eoin Kelly guided his county to All Ireland glory in 2010, ending Kilkenny's dream of a first ever five in a row. He was a brilliant leader. Henry Shefflin is one of the greatest hurlers ever to play the game and a man who holds a record 10 All Ireland senior hurling medals. He's also been hurler of the year three times. He is a King. Cork's Donal Óg Cusack is regarded as one of the finest goalkeepers ever to play the game. For the past 2 years he's worked as a coach with the Clare senior hurling team. In football, Tomás Ó Sé played for Kerry for 15 years. He was 'Footballer of the Year' in 2004 and is widely recognised as one of the best defenders ever to wear the green and gold. Pádraic Joyce is one of Galway's greatest ever footballers and was a member of the All Ireland winning side of 1998 and 2001.

Valerie Mulcahy is one of the most gifted footballers ever to play Ladies GAA. She won an incredible 10 All Ireland senior football medals with Cork.

In boxing, Kenny Egan is a man that won the heart of a nation in 2008 when he won an Olympic silver medal in Beijing. He's also achieved an incredible feat at home winning 10 Irish senior titles.

Eoin Reddan is a small man with a big heart. He represented Ireland 71 times and played for three different provinces throughout a hugely successful rugby career. Gordon D'Arcy is one of Ireland's greatest ever centres. He was also picked for the British and Irish Lions tour in 2005 and again in 2009.

In soccer, Damien Duff is widely regarded as one of the most talented footballers ever to wear an Irish jersey. He also enjoyed a hugely successful career in England.

Sonia O'Sullivan and Derval O'Rourke are two of Ireland's greatest ever athletes. Both from Cork, they beat off the best to become World champions. O'Rourke crushed the field in 2006 to win the World indoor title in the 60 metre hurdles. For nearly a decade, Sonia O'Sullivan was simply the best winning gold on the World stage. She also won a silver medal at the 2000 Sydney Olympics.

After retiring from rowing Gearoid Towey set up his own company in Australia called 'crossing the line sport.' It helps athletes before and after they retire. Towey won gold for Ireland at the 1996 and 2001 World championships.

For a non-Irish perspective, former English international rower and World champion Daniel Ritchie gives us his thoughts on life after sport. He sums up it up with a quote from boxing legend Sugar Ray Leonard.

"Nothing could satisfy me outside the ring. There is nothing in life that can compare to becoming a world champion, having your hand raised in that moment of glory, with thousands, millions of people cheering you on."

Niamh Fitzpatrick is one of the top psychologists in this country and has worked with some of the biggest names in Irish Sport. She gives us her expert opinion on life after sport.

I hope you enjoy the book.

Paul Byrnes

FOREWORD
MÍCHEÁL Ó MUIRCHEARTAIGH

I retired from broadcasting Championship, League games et al after the 2010 All Ireland Senior Football Final between Cork and Down. But in November of the same year I commentated on the International Rules Series match between Ireland and Australia.

I felt the time was right for me to retire then considering that a most enjoyable and absorbing adventure on Radio began for me away back in the final year of the Forties. It had been my life for over 60 years and I had enjoyed every single moment of it.

To retire wasn't really a very difficult decision at all in my case.

For many people retirement means a severance from a routine life style of work to which they have formed an attachment. As I see it retirement from such a work environment is much more difficult than situations like mine.

I was always going to games and events which could be thoroughly enjoyable and of course the added privilege of commentating on them. Both elements were complementary to each other and I was incredibly fortunate to see so many great players and witness so many incredible games. From provincial finals to All Ireland finals, it truly was a remarkable time. I was lucky enough to travel the world too and see our wonderful games played in Europe, Asia, The Americas and Australia. The GAA is a very special organisation and I feel so lucky to be still part of it today.

I might have been retiring from broadcasting but I certainly wasn't going to be retiring from being a spectator. So, in many ways nothing really changed for me. I go to as many or maybe even more games now than I ever went to when I was a commentator. Nothing beats 'hopping' into the car and heading off for the day enjoying something I love.

I enjoy them now in a different way. I'm free to be a supporter or spectator as situations change. Happily the enjoyment remains.

In my opinion people should never retire without having some kind of plan to deal with the new phase they are then entering. I've met people who retire and have nothing to look forward to or have no idea what to do next. And that just wouldn't be me. I avoided all that because of my love for sport and the love of going to games.

Retirement can hit some players hard. It can be very difficult for them after giving so much to their sport. Some decide for themselves when it's time to 'ease out'. But for others it is sometimes the case that a manager informs them that they may not be in his plans for the immediate future. That can sometimes be interpreted as the beginning of the end.

And that's it. It's over.

A huge chunk of their lifestyle is taken away from them in one block. They've been so used to going to work, going to training, playing matches and suddenly it's all over. It's never easy. They miss being part of something special.

An athlete's life certainly doesn't last forever. But they are not forgotten and personal memories remain as new stars emerge and now wear what was once 'your jersey'. How could it be easy? Most players accept it and realise that the current players are always the ones who claim the limelight. You've had your day. But you and many of your kind will soon be back taking some part in that 'Something Special'.

Go raibh maith agaibh uilig as uct bhur dílseacht agus dúthracht.

I think player welfare is hugely important, not just during a players' career but after their careers are over. Retirement is such a big change, a change that can overcome some people. It's just you now. That's why it's so important players receive proper guidance from organisations and others to help them adjust to life after serious active sport.

However, there is another side of retiring and that is the sense of freedom that invades the mind once you stop playing. You can now decide how you spend your time. You can now enjoy doing other things in your life. Your family sees a lot more of you and maybe like me continue going to matches and enjoying them not from the commentary box but from the stand.

Bainim sult agus taitneamh as agus gan amhras bíonn deis agam 'casadh leis na daone'.

HENRY SHEFFLIN

Kilkenny's Henry Shefflin is one of the greatest hurlers ever to play the game.

He won 10 All Ireland Senior hurling medals and 11 All Star awards. He was also named All Star Senior Hurler of the year three times and is the only player to hold such an honour.

From Ballyhale, Shefflin also captained his county to All Ireland glory in 2007.

To add to his collection, he won 13 Leinster Senior titles, 6 National hurling league medals and 3 All Ireland senior club crowns.

After a remarkable career, he retired in 2015 and is now a regular contributor on RTE radio and television. He's also a columnist with The Sunday Times.

He's married to Deirdre and they have five children, Sadhbh, Henry Jnr, Siun, Freddie and Tom.

"Henry got the absolute maximum out of his career. He left nothing behind."

BRIAN CODY

HENRY SHEFFLIN

At the time, retirement is a very difficult decision to make but it's probably just another stage in your life.

In my opinion, there are two types of people who retire: Those that want to and those that don't. I wanted to and knew it was the right thing for me.

It was a very daunting experience leading up to it. However, once I had made up my mind and announced it, it was much easier and almost a relief. I took my time considering it and was happy in my mind that it was the right decision. I haven't looked back since.

Before I retired, I spoke to some of my former teammates who had gone before me and chatted to them about their retirement. I've always been very close to Tommy [Walsh] and JJ [Delaney] who had both retired and they gave me a good insight into their experience. I knew it was coming so the main discussions as always were with my wife Deirdre and my family. I also had a good conversation with a great friend of mine, Brother Damien. I hugely respect his opinion and he's a man that would always give you the pros and the cons. I also had a long conversation with Brian [Cody] before preparing myself for the public announcement.

I didn't lie awake thinking about retirement, but I remember the night we won the All Ireland club title in March 2015 and chatting to Deirdre afterwards.

Instead of celebrating, I knew a decision had to be made regarding my retirement, so I spent the next few days thinking about nothing else bar that. I had put it off for long enough and it was time to put an end to all the rumours and speculation.

I didn't want to drag it out any longer, so I called a press conference in Kilkenny and announced that I was finally retiring.

I think most sportspeople really love what they do so understandably it can be hard to let go. That chapter in your life is gone, it's over. But I think the great thing about the GAA compared to other sports is that even when you retire from the inter-county scene you're not fully retired. You go back to your club and continue playing for a couple of years and you can kind a wind down. This isn't always the case in other sports where once it's over, it's over. So being a GAA player certainly helps in that sense.

Like most GAA players, you get up Monday morning and go to work. I can't imagine what it must be like for a professional sportsman or woman to retire and adjust to life after sport. You get up the following day and there's no more training, travelling or competing. It must be very difficult.

My last time to wear the black and amber of Kilkenny was the 2014 All Ireland Senior Hurling Final replay against Tipperary. It was a very different year for me because for the first time in my career I was no longer an automatic starter. My role that year was very different coming on in games with about 20 minutes to go but I never stopped believing that I could get back on the team and win a 10th All Ireland. The strength of our panel was always more important than any individual player.

The following March I was back in Croke Park again – this time with Ballyhale Shamrock's winning the All Ireland club title. I had made up my mind well in advance that I wouldn't decide on my future with the county team until after the club championship was over. And that's what happened. Winning the club title in Croke Park with my club was just fairy-tale stuff. I just couldn't ask for more. At 36, I had done it all, what more could I achieve.

Filling the void hasn't been a big issue for me, as I went back to the club after retiring from inter-county. However, the first year away from the county scene in 2015 was a bit odd as I didn't know what way to approach it. I also had to undergo an operation on my shoulder that year so it was somewhat of a distraction. 2016 was really my first full season away from the whole county scene so I approached the club like I had with the county team full on in training. I think some of that was to replace what I was doing for so long with the county. As a player you get to a point where your body is telling you one thing and your head another. Playing inter-county and playing with Kilkenny is high intensity stuff and extremely stressful on the mind never mind the body. You need to give yourself a chance and indeed think about the future before finally saying enough is enough.

I've replaced the void by spending more time with the family and focusing on my job with Bank of Ireland. If you've been successful in sport, you want to be successful in business as well. I love a challenge, I always have and for me now it's to develop my career even further and push on. Every inter-county player will tell you that playing GAA does stall your career. You can't push yourself too much because of the massive commitment involved at county level. When you retire you certainly then have the opportunity to do such. I think there's a lot to be learned from sport that can be applied to business as well.

You're always trying to improve, always trying to progress your career and always trying to get to a stage of happiness. When I retired I also got involved in the media as a lot of sportspeople do when they finish up. I started working with RTÉ and *The Sunday Game* as well as writing for *The Sunday Times.* And that helped hugely in retirement as you're at the games, you're still talking about the sport you love and you still feel very much part of it. I really enjoy working with The Sunday Game as it's such a big brand in Ireland and people associate it with the games themselves. It's interesting being on the other side of the game now and being a pundit.

I've had some amazing days. Winning my first All Ireland Senior hurling medal in 2000 against Offaly was great. 2007 was also very special as I was captain that day. Unfortunately, I went off at half-time after doing my cruciate. It was also an incredibly emotional day as James McGarry [whose wife Vanessa had died tragically in July that year] lifted the cup with me along with his son Darragh.

I really enjoyed 2012 as well and the final against Galway. We were up against it the first day but managed to get ourselves back into a game that looked lost. These are just games you dream of and want to be part of such. We won the replay comfortably.

However, my greatest day has to be our first county club title in 2006. I'd grown up in Ballyhale, I'd watched them win All Ireland's and now here I was with my friends and family capturing the title. It was always a dream of mine from day one and as a little boy behind the bar in Ballyhale where my parents ran the local pub. When I started playing, we weren't even a Senior team. We'd also lost the county final the year before so this was special. Incredibly special.

As a Kilkenny hurler, I was very fortunate to win a lot of titles and enjoy that winning feeling on a regular basis. When you win your first one it's just crazy and an out-of-body experience.

But after you win a few and you mature it's just a huge sense of relief and a feeling that you got there. All sportspeople know what it's like to win and what it's like to lose. There's such a difference. I always loved the dressing room after we won but I also enjoyed doing a lap of the pitch and celebrating with the fans. It was amazing to meet your family and celebrate with them too and enjoy a drink in the players' bar afterwards.

After that we'd get back on the bus and head for the hotel and the winners' banquet. And this is something I always remember about the bus. When you arrived in Croke Park earlier before the game you knew this was it now, we're here to do a job and hopefully everything will go well for us. And then when you get back on the bus afterwards with the Cup there's just a real sense of we've done it.

I've had tough days too, but they're all experiences in my view. 2010 was hugely disappointing after such a massive build up to that game. We were going for an historic five in a row and there was a huge amount of talk and media interest in relation to my cruciate, would I play or not... To be honest I was just glad when it was all over.

In 2013, I picked up another injury and it was just a bad year and a bad summer. To add to the misery, I got sent off in the All Ireland Quarter Final against Cork in Thurles. I felt very low at the time. It was my third year in a row getting injured in the last match of the year, I had a couple of surgeries, I'd spent a lot of time in hospital and was extremely frustrated. I felt I hadn't done myself justice, I'd tried too hard and over compensated for that and I felt I had let the lads down getting sent off. I remember the lads going for a few drinks after the game back in Kilkenny and I just hadn't the stomach for it. I texted Deirdre to pick me up from the bus and I went home and cut the grass that evening. It certainly was a year to forget.

The first year I lost an All Ireland was in 1999, when Cork beat us in the final on a very wet day in Croke Park. It was a horrible feeling, almost death like. It's funny it didn't hit me as much in 2010 despite losing out on a record five in a row. We were well beaten in the 2004 final against old rivals Cork which was also hugely disappointing but looking back now I was lucky because I won 10 of them and only lost 3. I've little to complain about.

In defeat Brian would always speak to us telling us the importance of keeping our heads up and moving on. There would be plenty of tears but different lads would deal with defeat in different ways. It's so quiet in a losing dressing room. You're just afraid to move, afraid to talk. Once Brian would say his few words you'd gather your stuff and head away. The hardest thing for me losing an All Ireland was returning to Kilkenny and over 20,000 fans in the city looking at you. You're standing there on stage thinking what are we doing here, we lost. I just wanted to go home and close the door behind me.

I miss the craic and the dressing room banter. You hear people these days saying there's no fun anymore, it's all got so serious. I don't agree. There's plenty of fun, you make your own fun. That's what I really miss. I miss the big days too. I miss the competitiveness of going into training and pushing myself and having someone pushing me along.

As time goes on I think more about my career and the great days I've had be it with club or county. I often think did we actually do that?

We felt we were just lads heading in and playing a game we loved. So as time goes on I just think of the great experiences we had, the places we visited, the stories we told and the fun we had along the way. It was an amazing journey. Life after sport is good.

GEAROID TOWEY

Gearoid Towey is a former Irish international rower. He was World rowing champion in 1996 and again in 2001. He also competed at three Olympic Games, Sydney 2000, Athens 2004 and Beijing 2008.

In 2005, he attempted to cross the Atlantic Ocean with his friend Ciaran Lewis in a 23-foot rowing boat. They were forty days at sea but after some incredibly bad weather and extremely difficult conditions their boat was pitch poled by a massive wave, leaving them adrift over 1,400 kilometres from land. They were rescued during a Force 9 storm at sea by a large tanker.

Originally from Cork, Gearoid has travelled extensively across the globe but now lives in Sydney, Australia and is the founder and CEO of an organisation called 'Crossing the Line Sport' which is dedicated to helping athletes deal with life during and after sport.

He speaks regularly about the subject in Australia and around the world.

"Gearoid was the most technical oarsman
I ever rowed with. He had the ability to improve
any boat he was in. On race day a different man
appeared and you saw how competitive he really was.
Off the water he's a loyal and lifelong friend."

SAM LYNCH

GEAROID TOWEY

I retired from rowing shortly after the Beijing Olympic Games in 2008. I knew I was retiring and couldn't wait. I left China on the Tuesday before the closing ceremony the following Sunday. My days as an International rower were over. Mentally, I just couldn't go anymore and physically I was tired, exhausted and totally burnt out. It was time to stop. Rowing is such a demanding sport. You're dieting from Christmas to the following September every year. Training is hard, competing even harder.

I was lucky to win several World championship medals but I still feel the Athens Olympics of 2004 was the one that got away. I was rowing with Sam Lynch and we felt it was our best chance to win an Olympic medal. We had a great relationship and totally trusted each other. When we didn't make the final, a part of rowing died for me. I found it so hard to come to terms with how you could work so hard and go so fast and still not get there. For any athlete that can be hard to get your head around. I really felt I'd had enough at that stage and decided to take a year off. However, being a rower—and the person I am—I kept training. That year [2005] my funding was cut which really irritated me. Just two years earlier, we had won a World bronze medal in Milan. I was so annoyed. I was in University at the time doing my degree and of course did the Trans-Atlantic challenge, which ended after 40 days at sea. But what an experience. Whenever I had a gap in International rowing I always loved doing adventure rowing. Taking on the Atlantic in a small boat was certainly an adventure. I'm glad I tried it and glad I did it.

It had a profound effect on my life going forward in a good way and in a bad way too. In a good way because I had taken on the mammoth challenge but in a bad way because I didn't process it. I just continued on when I got home and went straight back into life and that was definitely the wrong approach. I should have taken some time out and processed it all but hindsight is a great thing.

I kept training and went straight back into the Irish team winning at the World Cup and a bronze medal at the World Championships in Eton in 2006. I was joyful but didn't have the feeling of elation that I'd experienced in previous victories. I was top of the world in my sport at that time but it wasn't pushing all the buttons. There was something missing. I came home from the World championships that September and just slept for weeks. Sometimes up to 12/13 hours a day. I was so tired. After a decent break I went back training but found it really hard. Usually I'd be looking forward to it but I wasn't enjoying it and started to skip training for the first time. My times in training were way down and I felt I was also letting the team down. I was tired, burnt out and not enjoying the sport I'd loved but nobody including the coach at the time could see that one of his top athletes was in trouble. Away in training camp I decided that's it, I'm leaving and headed home thinking I'm probably never going to row again.

I took a break, finished my degree in college and went on a proper holiday for the first time in years. Hoping to qualify directly for the Beijing Olympics the Irish team finished outside the top 11 in the 2007 World Cup and so had to go through the qualifiers to make the Games the following year. A phone call followed from the sports council wondering would I return to the team and help them secure a place in Beijing.

I was living in Barcelona at the time and had just turned down a new office job which I knew didn't suit me. After much consideration, I returned to the boat and went back rowing with the Irish team. I felt rested and knew I could do it again. I felt I owed something to my teammates and what else was I going to do? I was back. However we failed to medal in Beijing.

I've had a very good career winning World Cups, World championships and numerous other titles. I was very driven from a very young age towards rowing and always felt I was going to do it. It was just in me. I had a tape of Lucerne and the 1990 championships and I must have watched it a thousand times. I remember the commentary to this day. It was ironic that when we won the World Championships in 2001 it was in that venue.

As a serious rower I set myself goals early in my career to make the Irish Olympic team and win a medal at the World championships. I achieved both very quickly [World Championships 1996 and the Sydney Olympic Games 2000] and so the bar was raised. What else could I achieve in rowing? I also won gold at the World Championships in 2001 and bronze in 2003 and 2006. All those medals mean a lot. It means we're in the history books forever.

The celebrations after our 2001 win were particularly special. We just had great craic. I ended up starting a snooker exhibition match between Ken Doherty and Jimmy White, I got invited to some great events, we drank plenty of beer and life was good.

Winning is just pure relief. For me it's a real case of thank god it's over especially if you're favourites as there is so much expectation. Another hugely enjoyable feat for me looking back on my career was winning the Australian National Championships shortly after Sydney 2000, which is a hard race to win. That was a great moment in my life. I'm also proud that I've won medals in both sculling [two oars] and sweep rowing [one oar]. You've got bar side which is to the left and stroke side which is to the right. It's very rare to have someone who can do both sides in rowing.

I've always felt that sport is a massive gamble. You put every ounce of yourself into something with no guaranteed outcome. My biggest disappointment in rowing is the fact that I went to three Olympics but didn't make the final. If we'd made the final in Sydney or Beijing it would have been a surprise but there was huge expectation in Greece. It still hurts. In sport, there are plenty of tough days be it a bad result, a serious injury or an unexpected operation. But I've always come through and kept going. I'm certainly not one to give up.

I've always loved Australia and spent a lot of time training and rowing there throughout the years. It's a great country. After retiring in 2008, I went travelling again and ended up in Sydney where I met my partner Maurice. We broke up but I remained in Australia and with my rowing days over I began to seriously think about life after sport.

In 2009, Irish boxer Darren Sutherland sadly died by suicide. I was with him in Beijing in 2008. He was such a great person and so dedicated to his sport. His death had a huge effect on me and I just couldn't digest it at all. I began to look at athlete's and their mental well-being. I began looking at athletes and life after sport.

I was lucky. My retirement was fairly text bookish. I wanted to retire, I was at the top of my game, I had a degree [BA in Natural Science] and I had a lot of interests outside of sport, yet I still found it tough at times. But what about athletes who retire from sport who don't have a degree, who don't have any outside interests? What do they do now? How will they manage the transition? I knew plenty of them [and many still involved in sport] and so began to seriously research the topic. I quickly found out there was very little material on it despite it being so important.

There wasn't a 'one stop shop' for athletes to go to if they had questions about life during sport or life after sport and needed answers. Back home in Ireland I got involved in organising events and enjoyed that for a period before returning to Australia once again. I was keen to get my transition in sport idea up and running so I went off and got some experience with Western Sydney Wanderers football club followed by the New South Wales Institute of Sport before I set up my own business 'Crossing the Line Sport.'

'Crossing the Line Sport' is a lifeline for athletes. It's about athlete wellbeing and retirement. Crossing the line sport is not affiliated to any sports organisation or governing body. It assists athletes of all levels around the world by offering a space online where they can share stories confidentially, receive advice from experts and any information relevant to athlete retirement. The service is run by athletes for anyone who has chased a sporting or performance dream, no matter what level they attained. Crossing the line sport believe preparation for the end of an athletic career should begin as soon as an athlete starts chasing their dream. Crossing the line sport also delivers effective workshops and seminars to help athletes become more self-aware, resilient and balanced.

A sorted human being makes a formidable performer. Far too many great people get stuck in no man's land when they retire from sport so this website 'Crossing the line sport' and workshops which we've presented in numerous places around the world help to educate current athletes and support retired athletes in all sports.

When I was an athlete the people I listened to most were other athletes because they had done it. They'd been through it. They had experienced it. Sporting federations don't really ask athletes to share their stories or their experiences so this is a big part of our website. We love to hear athlete's stories because we want to help other people.

Overall, there are a couple of strands to the organisation. First of all, there is the website which keeps the conversation alive. Secondly, we do workshops. We also look after teams on an ongoing basis, their well-being and we hold summits around the world including Dublin in 2016.

The biggest issues I find with athletes retiring are as follows;

PHYSICAL - When you stop training, your brain chemistry changes. One of the main reasons I got into sport in the first place was it made me feel good. When an athlete stops training and competing it can be physically challenging. Apart from the brain, the body is a big factor. All athletes are obsessed with their body, how they look, etc. I remember Sam Lynch and myself undergoing a body fat test and I was 5% and Sam was 5.1% and I called him 'fat' for two weeks. When you retire your body can change very quickly and a lot of athletes find it hard to deal with that.

COMMUNITY - Team mates will die for one another and spend years training, travelling and competing together. They are your community. Suddenly you retire and they aren't with you any longer. That can be very difficult to deal with.

DRIVE - That unquestionable drive that got you out of bed in the morning. Hail, rain or snow you got up in the dark at 5am and went training. I did it because it made me feel good. I knew that was my drug. When that's gone, it also be difficult.

IDENTITY - Your identity is hugely wrapped up in your sport. It's a big problem with athletes when they retire. They lose their identity. You start asking yourself what am I going to do? Who am I in the world? What am I going to be? What can I provide for people? All those questions with no answers. It can really damage your self-confidence. You look around and everybody else is moving on. You're behind for the first time in your life.

HELP — Athletes don't ask for help and it's a big problem. It's hard to expect somebody who's not programmed to ask for help to start suddenly asking for help. If I do need help, who do I talk to? I can't talk to my team because they've moved on. I can't talk to my friends or family because they just won't understand. They just think you've been living the dream.

When you retire, your family expects to get you back. They expect you to move on and be ok with retirement but that's not always the case. Drinking, gambling and divorce can be common occurrences. Therefore families need to be educated just as much as athletes. They need to understand life after sport. That's why 'Crossing the Line Sport' is there because athletes can talk to other athletes and those around you can also educate themselves about life after sport.

Our main contracted clients these days are current sports organisations where we deal a lot with prevention. We also now partner with another organisation in Australia called 'The Final Whistle'. They also help athletes during and after their sporting careers. They work with a lot of rugby teams and other sportspeople. Together we've produced and delivered a 'Sport to Life' programme which focuses on some key areas such as mental, physical, psychotherapy, career, etc. The idea is to get federations to pay for this programme for their athletes when they're retiring. Both 'Crossing the Line Sport' and 'The Final Whistle' are independent organisations.

The big problem I've found is that a lot of athletes don't engage with their existing welfare services because they're afraid anything they say will get back to the coach, so they say nothing. Therefore, we make it very clear to them that whatever you say to us is completely confidential.

We're never going to speak to the coach about anything unless you ask us to do so. That's one of our strengths.

When you're an athlete and you're competing at the highest level you have to go to a different place in my view. You have to go deep, really deep to a different place to get a big result. When that's not there or you're not willing to put yourself there then it's over. I can understand athletes who hang on, who keep going, who are prepared to sit on the bench because sport is a drug. It's been your life. But when I retired that was it, there was no turning back. I was lucky because I went past sport and developed so many other interests outside of that. I even went to drama school for a year.

Finally, if you think what you're doing right now is the hardest thing in the world, then be prepared because real life is a lot harder. Here's an analogy: A young footballer is on trial with Manchester United and you offer him a full-time contract. However, the deal is that when you're finished, you have to go live in Mongolia for the rest of your life. What's it to be? The kid goes "I'll take the contract." So, to prepare himself for life after football and life in Mongolia he goes there during off season, he spends time there, he starts to learn the language so he's ready when his career at Manchester United comes to an end. It's just so important to prepare for life after sport, because when you retire as a sports person you might as well be going to Mongolia because life is so different.

DERVAL O'ROURKE

Derval O'Rourke retired from international athletics in 2014. She is a former World sprint hurdles champion.

She has also represented Ireland at 3 Olympics: Athens 2004, Beijing 2008 and London in 2012.

O'Rourke won gold in the 60-metre hurdles at the 2006 World Championships in Moscow, becoming the first Irish woman to win an indoors medal. That same year the Cork athlete finished joint second at the European Championships in the 100-metre hurdles.

In 2009, she captured a bronze medal in the 60-metre hurdles at the European Indoor Championships in Italy. Derval finished 4th at the World Outdoor Athletics Championships in 2009. A year later, she added another medal to her collection winning a silver award at the European Championships in Barcelona.

She picked up another bronze in the 60-metre hurdles in Gothenburg at the 2013 European Indoor Championships.

Derval lives in Cork with her husband Peter and daughter Dafne.

"Derval was the ultimate championship performer. Her best times and Irish records were set on a European or global stage"

JERRY KIERNAN

DERVAL O'ROURKE

Since I retired, life has been busy. As a professional athlete, I was always very focused and didn't let anything distract me from running well. Therefore, I was good at saying no to everything like weddings, birthdays, parties, going on holidays.... I was also very strict in what I did for sponsors. It's funny, people always thought I was away doing warm weather training which was always a great excuse but the reality is I was training here in Ireland in the wind and rain and totally focused on athletics. It was my life.

I've a new life now and its different altogether. I have a start up business focusing on health and fitness, I've become a mother and we've built a new house in Crosshaven. It's almost like I'm making up for the years I wasn't here because when you're competing on the international stage you just haven't the time to do other things. It's all about surviving, competing and winning.

I've never struggled with retirement and certainly don't feel like there's a void in my life since I finished up. I now have a different focus, with my new business and being a mum. I've always been someone who likes to do things well, and like with athletics, I'm very results driven in business. I'm always looking at the targets for the next six months and then looking at what are the targets for the year and going after them. I guess there's just a side to me that likes to do things this way. I've always been very driven and just love getting results. Since I started my own business I've also taken on some employees which is a big thing for me personally. I dedicated my life to athletics for a long time and now I'm dedicated to this new venture which for me is a place where myself and my team can inspire people and share simple ways to live a fitter and healthier lifestyle. Everything in the business comes back to my core message which is to 'eat well and keep moving.'

Throughout my career, I was good at both these things to get results. I think everybody should eat well and exercise no matter what they do.

You only have one life, so it's hugely important to be as healthy as possible so you can enjoy it.

On the corporate side of the business, we go into company spaces and do a lot of bespoke events. Long term, I'd like my business to become one that people would recognise as something that's a solution to a much healthier lifestyle. However, like any new business, there's long hours and it can be tough going at times but it's a new buzz for me and I'm very excited. I would hate in 5 years time that people still only knew me as being an athlete. I hope I would have achieved other things in life to be remembered by.

I retired in June 2014, but nobody knew I was about to retire except for the people closest to me. The Sports Council and Athletics Ireland didn't know. I had surgery on my achilles the year before and I felt under pressure to get back quickly from the operation. But that all changed one day on a trip with my husband Peter. It was early in the day because anytime I was away I always wanted to be back home for training. I had always put training first ahead of everything. It was eleven months since the surgery and my achilles was killing me. I knew I had a lot of work to do to get back to where I wanted to be but I also knew the Federation wouldn't give me that time and would also cut my funding. I was now in my early thirties and just didn't have the energy or will to hustle as I would have had at 21 so I was very practical and just said to Peter 'there's no rush, we're in no hurry back home, I'm done with this.' I spent the following 2 weeks planning my exit strategy and spoke to Sean and Terrie Cahill [my coaching team for nearly 10 years] who were on the same page as me. 'It's time to walk away, it's just how you do it, announce it.' they said. They seemed happy that I had made the right decision.

My last proper race was the European Indoor Championships in 2013 where I finished 4th and the fastest I'd run in 7 years. I also ended up being upgraded to bronze from that race as the winner tested positive for drugs. It's bittersweet because the medal didn't arrive in the post for over two years even though I knew within two weeks of the competition that the winner had tested positive. Retiring just felt right. I wrote a piece for the newspaper announcing my retirement from athletics and that was it. I always wanted to retire in my own way and announce it through the article and a tweet and that's what I did.

I had a brilliant team around me but I was always a bit of a lone wolf too and never really engaged too much with the likes of Athletics Ireland and the Sports Council. The only official thing I did was tell the drug testers. I got an email back from them shortly after I retired to say if I was coming out of retirement I had to give them 6 month's notice.

I was 33 when I retired from athletics. I went to 3 Olympic Games [Athens 2004, Beijing 2008 and London 2012], 5 indoor and outdoor World Championships, won 5 major medals including a World Indoor gold in 2006 and I just wasn't hungry anymore. I was also tired of trying to manage the financial side of being an athlete. Your income was entirely dependent on how you raced and if you were injured or sick then you were going to be pretty broke.

I think retiring from a team is different in many ways to retiring from a sport that is just you and you only. Athletics is a very selfish sport to be in as it all rests on you. I also couldn't ask my coaches [Sean & Terrie] for any more. They had given nearly 10 years of their lives to helping me get to this stage and all for the love of the game. They never got paid, it was all voluntary and I just couldn't justify asking for a second more of their time for my dreams. For me it was easy because it was taking pressure of them. They had three children, they had a business and they had their own life.

I can see how a lot of people struggle with retirement but I also think [not wanting to sound harsh] that you have to take responsibility for your own life. Nobody's career lasts forever and retirement is inevitable. At the end of the day, it's just so important to have some kind of plan in place. I was lucky. I competed at the Olympics in 2004 and if I had picked up a serious injury at that stage, I would have had a degree to fall back on.

At the start of every year while competing as a professional athlete I would sit down with a pen and paper and write down on one side my plan for the track. For example, if it was a World Championship year what do I want to achieve, what's my goal?. On the other side of the page the headline would be 'off track' and what's the one thing I'm going to do away from athletics this year that will benefit me long term. I was always looking at the end game. So, I think the people that struggle are the people who don't have a plan. Then again perhaps I didn't enjoy my career enough as much as others as I was always looking at life after sport. I was never relaxed because I always had a sense that it could end at any time.

I probably never lived in the moment as I was always thinking about tomorrow. I ran my fastest ever in 2010 and three weeks later I was handing in my thesis as part of the Masters in Business Management course I did at the Smurfit Business School. I spent little if any time celebrating but that was me. As I competed, in between I was also writing and thinking about school. I was always thinking about the future and what would I do next.

I felt that when it came to athletics, you're very disposable. I had seen that from a young age to some of the best in the business. As soon as they started to struggle they were very easily replaced with the next big thing. I promised myself that I would never find myself in that position and so always protected myself from that. A lot of sportspeople find it hard to walk away. In the end, it was an easy decision for me to retire as I am and always have been very practical.

When I was 24, I had already made an Olympics [Athens 2004] and had made all the major championships but I'd never got out of a Semi-Final. I had just finished college [The Smurfit Business School] and everybody was applying for big jobs in the likes of PwC and other big companies. It was 2005, the celtic tiger had gripped the nation and here was I making a minimum wage as an athlete. I wasn't a professional athlete because I wasn't making enough money to do such. It was a difficult time for me. I rang Sean Cahill, whom I barely knew, but I really respected [Sean represented Ireland at sprint hurdles at the 1996 Olympics in Atlanta] and asked him if he'd come out to the track for a night and watch me hurdle. I needed someone to be totally honest with me. This was make or break for me. If I wasn't good enough I'd walk away from athletics and go down the business route. Sean said he didn't coach but I wasn't asking him to coach me, I was asking him for his opinion. Thankfully he agreed to come out for 1 hour to give me his honest assessment but he was adamant 'that's it'. After the session, he told me I was rubbish at hurdling and could be so much better if I just changed a few things. I wrote down everything he said to me on a notepad that same evening and my plan was to go away and work on all after that. To my surprise he turned to me before he left and said I'll see you next Tuesday and that was the start of a great relationship that would last until I retired. He had a very successful electrical company with a big team under him so he was already a very busy man but thankfully he agreed to coach me. With Sean came Terrie his wife and they became my coaches.

Six months later, I won the World Indoors.

I'm so glad I made that phone call. Prior to that I thought I'd over exceeded a little bit with going to the 2004 Olympics, etc so if he had said you've totally maxed out and walk away from it now I would have accepted it, I'm very practical like that. Instead, it brought me on a journey I only dreamed about as a child and many amazing moments that I will treasure for the rest of my life.

My greatest day as an athlete was at the World Championships in Berlin in 2009 where I finished 4th in the 100m hurdles. As a young athlete growing up in Cork I was never someone that was picked out as a junior, I was never someone that stood out from the crowd. I went from being that person to winning a World Championship gold medal in 2006 to a terrible year at the Olympics in 2008 where I was sick and thought seriously about retirement. I just hated the sport at that time. I thought it was a horrible place, I thought it was too hard.

And then I rolled the dice and changed a few things and started enjoying it again in 2009. At that stage, I'd lost all my sponsors so in many ways the pressure was off me. I was earning little or no money. I was funding my athletics off sponsorship money I had saved. I started to pick races I liked and wanted to go to and had direct flights. That always helped as did having Paul [Hession] and David [Gillick] with me. I trained very hard that year, I started going out with Peter [who I married in 2013] and I was just happier. I went into the 2009 World Championships with little or no pressure. I thought what's the worst that can happen? The worse that could happen was the Olympics the year before when I was good enough to win a medal. When I look back on my career now that's the one that got away. Lining up in that final in Berlin in 2009 I really thought genuinely I was going to win despite being ranked 24th at that time. I finished 4th and was delighted. I celebrated hard. Few people think of that performance but it was huge for me.

We [my coach Sean and Irish athlete Thomas Chamney who competed in Berlin] ended up in McDonald's at 4am that following morning and talked about the comeback for hours from the heartbreak of Beijing to the brilliance of Berlin.

It was my greatest day.

It was why I became an athlete. I loved to run, I loved to race and I loved to show the girls that I could match them and at times beat them when the stakes were high. All I ever wanted in athletics was a chance and that day in Berlin I got a chance and took it. I ran the fastest race of my life and was so happy. Funny enough the result didn't come up for ages so in cases like that you start making deals with the devil.

I remember going 'please let it be top 3' as I stared at the board. It felt like hours. In athletics they always put the winner up first, then second and so on so you're just standing there hoping, praying for a place on the podium. I knew I was in the mix and I knew I was in with a real shout. In the end I'd finish 4th as the official scoreboard lit up the Berlin sky.

But I remember thinking that's unbelievable. I've just ran 12.67 for the first time in my life. I was the happiest 4th place ever because it was massive for me personally after the previous 12 months. I had come from a horrible place to a great place in my life again. Athletics was once again a simple sport despite all those outside my circle who were telling me differently. You run from A to B as fast as you possibly can over 100 metres and jump a few hurdles and I'd made it really complicated. It was far from complicated.

Just minutes before that race I asked Sean what's the plan? He replied laughing 'definitely don't embarrass us' and then on a serious note he said 'run like fuck and there will be very few people in front of you'. That was the plan and that's what I did. That day it was about running from A to B and as fast as I could. That was my best day, and way better than any of my medal days. It was simply amazing.

In sport, there are plenty of tough days and I've had my fair share of them in athletics.

In fact, I ran so many races and rarely ran well because I was a real championship performer. I had a couple of brutal days none more so than the 2008 Olympics in Beijing where I totally bombed. It was just horrendous. To be honest in the build up to it I never thought it was going to go well for many reasons. I went to the UK the year before to train which I had convinced myself was the right thing to do. Turns out it was an idiotic decision. I was miserable and I knew nobody over there. I wasn't obsessed or anything like that in relation to winning an Olympic medal but I was just in a bad place and it got worse 4 weeks out from the Games when I tore my groin warming up at the Nationals. Tweaking a groin when you're trying to jump hurdles is a disaster. The chances of seriously competing for an Olympic medal were over.

I also felt like everybody was watching me, talking about me and analysing me and I was very uncomfortable with the whole situation. Looking back I simply dealt with the pressure badly. And then, I bombed in Beijing.

It was quite sad but my overall emotion was anger as I had dramatically changed how I always approached the sport in the 12 months build up to those Games. I'd gone from being someone who was self-driven and in control to someone who was easily influenced. I had people telling me you should be doing this and doing that, it would be great for your profile, etc when deep down I knew it was bullshit. I wasn't doing athletics for the profile, I was doing it to run as fast as I could and leave the sport knowing I had given it everything. I had got distracted and was angry at myself. I also felt I'd let my team [Sean and Terrie] down. They deserved a lot more than that 2008 Olympic performance. I felt I had let Sean down who had left his wife, three children and his business behind to travel to Beijing and be by my side. I was so angry with myself and knew I was better than that. I sat in the stand and watched the final. I'd always make myself watch finals that I didn't make because I always felt I'd learn something from watching it up in the stand as you can't when you're down amongst the girls on the track. I was always interested to see if there was something I could do better and improve my own performance and technique. Plus watching a final I wasn't in was huge motivation for winter training, I brought that hurt into the hard tough training sessions. No training session is ever as hard as sitting in a stand watching a final. Watching that final in 2008, I really felt afterwards that there was little to be scared of and that I could have been amongst the medals on the day. The time I ran in Berlin a year later would have medalled so I was right, I was that good. But Beijing was a low point in my career. Looking back on it now some years later and retired it doesn't feel as bad as it actually was at the time.

There were other dark days too.

I finished 4th at the 2013 European Indoors but I was just incredibly frustrated at the sport that day because I felt Turkish athlete Nevin Yanit was taking a bucket load of drugs. And here was I working my arse off to try and win a medal.

I knew no way it this legit and felt very disillusioned. As I watched the medal ceremony I just thought the whole thing stinks. I'd no problem people beating me who were better than me, it happened all the time but not in this way.

I don't miss the stress. I miss funny things like justifying going to the gym for three hours something I just can't do now. I have a family, I have a business, etc. When I was in shape I was in great shape, I just felt so physically fit and could dedicate time to my recovery strategy. I do really miss being that fit and justifying spending time being that fit. Time is a massive privilege when you're an athlete. As a full time athlete you have so much time to yourself. Yes, it's a great lifestyle and I enjoyed it but it came with a huge amount of stress. I always put myself under a massive amount of pressure to perform because I always wanted to justify being in it. Some athletes do it for the lifestyle but are generally not the ones that win medals but I did if for one reason – to win medals and perform far better than anyone expected.

I always felt that this life had to deliver medals and at the end of the year there had to be a reason for why I was doing this. I always set extremely high standards for myself. Yes, other athletes probably enjoyed the journey a lot more than I did but at the end of the day I had more medals.

Now that I've retired I consider it a massive privilege to have had the career and life I've had to date. Sometimes I hear people who've retired complaining about numerous things including drugs in sport, injuries etc. I could give out about drugs but at the end of the day if you take everything into account and what I got from the sport, the doors that it opened, the things that I did, it was indeed a huge privilege. It has given me massive opportunities.

I got to travel the world and got to compete at the highest level. I got to stand on the podium with a World championship gold medal around my neck. I started travelling at 17, when I was still in school. While most of my age was heading off on a family holiday I was heading to Eastern Europe to run.

To do that while growing up through the sport and have a load of kit sponsors who are paying you to wear their clothes it was ridiculous. Ridiculous in a great way. You were running for your town, your county and your country. People were so interested and so supportive. It was just a massive honour.

GORDON D'ARCY

Gordon D'Arcy is a former Irish rugby player who retired from the game in 2015.

He won two RBS 6 Nations titles with Ireland including the Grand Slam in 2009. D'Arcy also travelled on two British & Irish Lions tours. He also won three Heineken Cup titles with Leinster.

He made his Irish debut against Romania in the 1999 World Cup and went on to win 82 International caps with his country.

He was the RBS 6 Nations player of the year in 2004 as Ireland captured their first Triple Crown in 19 years.

Gordon lives in Dublin with his wife Aoife, daughter Soleil and son Lennon.

"Gordon D'Arcy was one of the most talented centres ever to play for Ireland. While playing in the shadow of the great Brian O'Driscoll his role in the success of the Irish team was often underestimated. With O'Driscoll he forged one of the greatest centre partnerships in the history of modern rugby."

EDDIE O'SULLIVAN

GORDON D'ARCY

As I headed West, I knew that phone call was coming. A conversation that would end one amazing journey.

Shortly after the RBS 6 Nations in 2015, I announced my retirement from rugby. I was in the 35-man squad for the competition that year but didn't play any act or part in it. Despite that, my ambition was still to go after the World Cup but it didn't play out that way.

Every player gets judged by the same yardstick. I had a game to play in the friendly leading up to that World Cup but didn't play well. I was dreadful. That was my audition to get picked for the squad and get on that plane, but it didn't happen. I was absolutely past my peak, so I if I was going I was going as a squad player and I fully understood that. Looking back at the video, I knew I hadn't played well. I was willing but the body just wasn't there. I was very cathartic, very relaxed. So I got into the car and headed to the West of Ireland to join my wife and her family. They were surprised to see me but I explained the situation and that it was all but over. Shortly after that, Joe rang me with the news I expected and that I wouldn't be going to the rugby World Cup. To be fair to Joe, he doesn't enjoy giving bad news to anybody so I cut the conversation short by saying there'd be much tougher phone calls for him to make and that was it. I was now a retired rugby player just two weeks before the squad was officially announced for the 2015 World Cup. It was the full stop in my career. It was never going to define me or wasn't going to break me but it was ambitious to get to another World Cup.

It was great to be in the West and being able to think about things. Everybody, of course, was asking me was I ok. And I was fine. Of course, it would have been great to go and play in another World Cup even if only for a few minutes, but close second was playing in a game and realising I wasn't able to do it anymore largely before everybody else would feel it.

I was now a retired rugby player.

When you're playing rugby, you're very much in the moment so you don't really ever think about life after sport.

At 28 I broke my arm in 8 places, broke my wrist in 3 places and underwent numerous operations. Being injured gave me a lot of time to think, as I was in a holding pattern. I wasn't getting any better, I wasn't getting any worse, I couldn't train fully and I certainly couldn't play. It was so frustrating. All I could do is train 3 days a week to keep my fitness up and do some weights. Every couple of weeks I would go back for an x-ray and continue with my recovery. I had just gone back to college [UCD] to do Economics, but being unable to take notes was incredibly difficult and I had no choice but to take a step back from it. However, I did complete it a couple of years later as I continued playing rugby with both Leinster and Ireland. I found juggling a professional rugby career with college was fine. It's only difficult if you don't really want to do it and don't want to be there. So instead of going for coffee with the lads I would sit down and study for two hours. Completing that course gave me a serious kick into the real world. I got a chance to do some work experience with Investec at that time and a conversation started about life after rugby, working there, etc. I ended up getting a job with them so there was certainly a nice symmetry to having a full time job to go to after my rugby career ended.

I probably played the best game of my life at 33 years of age. Apart from one dropped ball, it was the most complete game I've ever played. I finally understood rugby, a game I truly love.

I think every athlete has a moral responsibility to themselves to think about life after sport. If you're an International athlete, or the best in your field, you will have spent all your life superbly prepared for everything you go into, trying to perceive problems before they come. So how much of a contradiction would it be to finish your career and not be ready for the next bit. It's your prerogative to be thinking about it particularly in the later years of your sporting career.

You don't have to know exactly what you're going at following your retirement but at least have options. The only certainty after professional sport is uncertainty. I've spoken to a lot of ex-players who in my view have managed their retirement from sport well. People like Shane Horgan, Denis Hickie and Malcolm O'Kelly have all gone on to enjoy great careers after rugby.

Retiring from rugby at 35 meant I'd gone through three different generations of rugby players. There were the people who were amateur who had started playing professionally. Then there were people my age group who played and then there were the new generation coming through. As one of the older and experienced players in the group in recent years, I did feel like the old man a little bit. I would go home to my wife and daughter while many of the younger lads would be heading out socialising. The commonality between the young and old was rugby, that's it.

When I retired, I didn't miss training and I certainly didn't miss the gym. I loved being on the pitch and I loved playing games. It's never easy to retire and walk away from a sport you love, but I happily accepted it. I wasn't looking over my shoulder and wondering was there one more game in me. That never entered my head at any stage. If anything it was a case of "did I play one too many"? But I knew that was it for me and had given it everything.

I do miss the craic with the lads. There's certainly no comparison between the banter in the dressing room and the office. It's very different. I've always found that in rugby and in team sport the teams that are successful are those people who live what they say and the people who don't live what they say within a successful culture in sport invariably don't last very long.

I played rugby but it never defined me as a person. I always felt very privileged to play the sport but in many ways it's a transition. The jersey is timeless but you only have it for a certain time.

You're just trying to do it justice. They didn't retire the number with me. I didn't get to bring it with me. I've always felt that defining yourself as a rugby player limits you. There are so many other possibilities out there.

If I still consider myself a rugby player at forty-five years of age then the balance isn't right there. I always said during my career that I'm not a rugby player, I'm a guy who plays rugby.

The biggest thing I miss about being a rugby player is the lifestyle. Apart from all the pressure that comes with it, finishing training [and you might have had a crap day] and coming home to your wife and children all smiling is just the greatest. Nothing in the world beats that.

With my new job, I try to get home before my children go to bed so at least I can put the key in the door to see that my daughter is the other side, pulling at the handle and just so excited to see me come home. It's just brilliant. I look forward to the weekends and spending time with the family. Life as a rugby player is a very active life. Your time is not your own. It's a very structured life and very definitive. You know you're in at 7am on Monday morning and finished at 5pm. You know you have physiotherapy at 3pm on Wednesday and that's it. Thursday is a day off. Friday is the captain's run. You have a lot of time to work with when you're a professional rugby player whereas now you don't have a lot of time and you're trying to build stuff in around it. It can be difficult at times to move from that active lifestyle where time is not your own to a new lifestyle where again time is not your own but you're also trying to cram other stuff into that time.

Filling the void of training, travelling and competing has been easy. I work between 55 and 70 hours a week in an office. I have two young children and a dog that needs to be walked every night. I write a weekly article for a newspaper and if I want to get to the gym it's before work in the morning or late in the evening. It's very easy to fill every hour on the clock.

Am I enjoying life after rugby? I don't know. I don't miss rugby. I still watch it as a fan. I'm not critical. I look at guys playing my position and go thank God I'm not playing now. Would I last in the modern game? As rugby is such a contact sport, unsurprisingly, my body has taken a lot of physical abuse over the years. So rather than waiting for a slipped disk at forty-five, I'm getting extensive physio now to help with it.

I'm also hoping to take up cycling and enter some competitions. That competitive edge will always be in me.

I had a very low expectation of what life outside rugby was going to be. I'm happy, I have a really good job, a great family, but I think the death of Dan Vickerman in Australia really made me aware that there are pit falls after you leave the game. There's definitely a piece missing from me since I retired. Whatever that piece is, I haven't found it yet. I really miss the competitive nature of sport and setting goals, the short timeframes.... I could wake up in the morning and do a great training session, which would in turn set me up for the big game at the weekend. You feel on top of the world. Timelines in the corporate world are very different. You talk to a client, you hear nothing for a month, then there's another meeting and six months could go by before you get anywhere. At the end of the day you mightn't even get a result. I struggle with that. Time moves a lot slower in the corporate world. There isn't that real competitive element in such as there is in sport. I really miss that.

I don't enjoy going to games. I feel like I shouldn't be there. I've spoken to a lot of the lads who have retired and they all agree that after a certain amount of time passes, you do feel a little more comfortable. There is a difference between being in the bubble looking out and the lens you look through after you retire. There is no comparison. I do a bit of commentary and enjoy it. You're up high and have a great view of the game, the movements and the tactics. If there was one piece of advice I could give to an athlete retiring or close to retiring that would be 'get moving'. There's no wrong decision. The worst thing you can do is make no decision. Your first job outside of rugby doesn't have to be perfect. It's easier to find a job when you have a job. Just make a decision.

Staying in rugby is the easy thing, getting out of rugby is the hardest. There are only so many jobs in the rugby world. Indecision is the biggest killer. The weeks and months afterwards can just slip by very quickly. The ex-rugby players network is just incredible. Players are just so generous with their time.

When I look back on my career now I don't really segregate the bits and pieces in it, what were my greatest moments. After all, it's a team sport. It's a team trophy. Winning the Grand Slam in 2009 was incredible, but I don't hold it in higher esteem to winning the Heineken Cup or the Pro12.

By picking out a Grand Slam I feel you don't do justice to other things such as my first cap, coming back from injury, first tackle I did after breaking my arm, winning in France or bringing my daughter to my last game. It was a lovely career and an honour to play it. I played with incredible guys and there were certainly more ups then downs. I enjoyed winning but I always felt as soon you win you don't want to get carried away and so you're shutting yourself down. Like cop on. I always had a healthy view of winning. It helps you develop a really healthy attitude to losing. I always felt that every time we lost it was another opportunity to get better. Every win was built on all the failures gone by. When we lost it was a case of figuring out what went wrong and making sure we didn't do it again.

When you play rugby for 18 years there are going to be plenty of tough days too.

The graph certainly goes up and down. I went from being on top of the world in 1999, when I won my first cap coming on as a substitute against Romania in the Rugby World Cup, to losing my contract with Leinster.

I also sustained plenty of injuries along the way too, including tearing my hip and breaking my arm. However, I enjoyed the screw ups and the testing periods along the way because in my view that's what makes you. That's what makes your character. If it's always easy then how do you judge yourself when the pressure comes on. I certainly learned more in the tough times than I did in the good times.

I would like to return to rugby at some stage in the future. There are a couple of boys' schools in my area where I live, so I'd love to coach schools. I'd love to coach an underage group and see them grow. It also be a good way to see if it's about the coaching or about the players. It would be great to have them for a number of years coaching them, teaching them and developing them.

I'd also love to be a manager someday. Not a head coach, like Joe, but a team manager, like Mick Kearney or Paul McNaughton who looked after Ireland in the past. I think I'd enjoy the position, as you're not involved in team selection or coaching but you still work very closely with the players in a different capacity.

However, I know I've a lot of ground to cover between now and then.

PÁDRAIC JOYCE

Pádraic Joyce is a former Gaelic footballer with Galway. He won 2 All Ireland Senior football titles and 3 All Star Awards.

He also won 6 Connacht titles in the maroon and white captaining his county to victory in 2008.

Joyce was top scorer in the 2001 All Ireland Senior football championship. He was also named Texaco Footballer of the Year.

He captained Ireland to International Rules success in 2004 with victory over Australia.

Padraic lives in Tuam, County Galway with his wife Tracey and children.

"Padraic was always inspired by
the big occasion rather than frightened by it,
evidenced by his clinical goal in the 1998 final
and his second half performance in 2001.
A true winner."

JOHN O'MAHONY

PÁDRAIC JOYCE

I knew it was coming. You always know that it's coming. But you always try and leave the sport first and foremost in the best way you can and try and get out of it on your terms. It doesn't always happen that way. At the start of 2012, I thought long and hard about going back or not that year. There was a new man at the helm in Alan Mulholland and he was making noises around the place that he would be making changes and bringing in some fresh blood. However, I still felt I'd something to give and so committed to another year of inter county football with Galway. I had recently started a new business PJ Personnel in the middle of the downturn and it was starting to take off. I was now working for myself so it meant a lot of early starts and late-night finishes. My day would consist of getting up at 5am to be in Dublin for 7am. Then home for training, followed by paper work, bed and then up again the following morning. The body was getting older, sorer and I was getting tired a lot quicker.

Being a county footballer is a huge commitment, coupled with the massive effort required to run your own business. I met Alan [Mulholland], Galway Senior football manager, at the time and we discussed the year ahead and my role. I would no longer be in the starting fifteen but would play a part in proceedings. However, my ambition was to play my way back into the first team. I found the year incredibly frustrating to be honest because I felt I could contribute a lot more than just 15 or 20 minutes here and there.

All through my career, I had always started games even if I wasn't one hundred percent fit. I always felt that even if I was only half fit I was more valuable than somebody fully fit.

As a sub I felt I was just going into quench fires. If the game was going well I didn't have a huge amount to do and if it wasn't I'd be under pressure to go in and perform miracles within that time frame.

I was never the best trainer in the world, I would always try and do enough but come match day, I would thrive on it and give it everything. I found the last year very hard with it all coming to an abrupt end against Antrim in the qualifiers.

I knew that morning we were struggling and I certainly wasn't happy with the preparations for the game. I came on for the last 10 minutes in Belfast but felt I could have given at least a half an hour despite carrying an injury picked up in training. We lost the game, which meant we were out of the 2012 championship and my days in the maroon and white were over. It was time to go. Indeed, I had made up my mind earlier in the year that 2012 would be the final year. I was going well in training and playing well in games but I was only playing a 'bit role' overall. It was terribly frustrating and at times during the year I often felt like walking away but I kept going. No player is bigger than the county, you do what you can for the maroon jersey but I had to make a decision about my career. Leaving your sport can be an incredibly hard and indeed emotional decision. As an inter-county player you're training a number of times during the week. In between all that, you're doing your own gym stuff and other things. I would wake up Monday morning, head to Dublin for an early meeting and spend the day in the capital. I would train in Galway on Tuesday followed by Dublin on Wednesday for more meetings. I would train again on Thursday in Galway before returning to Dublin again on Friday. And after all that, you would have a match on the Sunday. You certainly put most of your life on hold when you're playing for your county be it your family, career, etc. However, I found it very hard to step away from it.

I don't miss the winter training but when the league comes back around followed by the summer championship you really miss it. You're just gutted that you're no longer involved, no longer part of something you've belonged to for so long. You're outside the camp. Watching the games, you still feel you could give something. But it's over and it's hard to accept. I always loved playing for Galway and was always so proud of my club Killererin. I loved heading into Tuam or Galway for big games. I loved the buzz, the excitement, the intensity that goes with playing inter-county football. You'd give an arm for the boys you're playing with, it meant that much.

I remember going into Tuam for a Connacht league game shortly after I retired and standing in the terrace with my wife Tracey. I found that very hard and was almost in tears watching it.

I also missed going to training and filling that void was difficult at the beginning. So much so that I often considered going in to watch training but I decided not to in the end. I was no longer part of the Galway set up, I was gone and I didn't want to be a bug hanging around the place. You just have to remove yourself from it. When I'd go to games I would go to the opposite side of the stand just to be in a quieter spot. It took me a long time to get used of retirement. Yes, I was still playing with my club but it wasn't the same.

I got plenty of advice from people before I retired. I wouldn't say I took the advice but you would have a lot of people telling you what to do. Three years before I retired, I remember a friend of mine saying to me 'you should go now, make sure it's your decision and don't get dropped by a manager.' My father Paddy, who sadly passed way in 2015, was one of the main reasons why I played the game and always said 'play as long as you can while you can. You'll be long enough at home.' And obviously when I retired, I knew exactly what he meant.

At the same time, it's important not to overstay your welcome. There comes a time when younger players are going to take your place and you just have to accept that as well. I always felt you do what you can for the younger players coming through by encouraging them and giving them advice.

I miss the big days. I miss the buzz of the championship. I miss the week of a championship game and the big match build up. I miss the tactical meetings of how you're going to play the opposition and how you're going to try and beat them. When you retire you're now on the outside and guessing what's happening inside. I loved being part of the big plan.

I loved getting on the bus and going to matches. I also loved the journey because you never knew where you were going to end up. It was so exciting. You could end up being part of something very special like that of 1998 and 2001.

Every year started with hope and that's why I continued playing for so long, because you always thought this could be the year. You had to believe that and give it everything.

Over the last couple of years, I've been able to fill that void a lot easier. I'm married with children and running my own business which is hugely time consuming. The up-side of retirement is being able to spend more time with your family and being able to go away on holidays when you want to and not determined by the league or championship calendar. You miss out on so much while playing from birthday parties to weddings.

It's such a big change to go from being an inter-county footballer to retiring. You have no choice but to try to adapt. I still go to the gym twice a week to keep fit.

It's so hard to remove yourself totally from football. I still have ambitions to go into management someday but not at the moment as I have too many commitments with a young family and my business. I think most players would like to stay involved in sport in some capacity after they retire but there are only so many jobs in management or coaching...

Like many sportspeople, I'm now involved in the media and do some work with RTÉ radio, which I enjoy. I would go to the games anyway. But it is an honour to be asked by them to cover the game and they obviously value my opinion. I'd be huge into the tactical side of games and I find myself going to games earlier and earlier these days as I enjoy watching teams warm up. You see the different strategies, the different drills, the difference in warm ups. Dublin, for example, spends most of their warm up practicing their shooting skills and kicking at the goal.

There has been a couple of memorable days playing for Galway, with 1998 certainly one of them. On the bus home the following night after winning that All Ireland we came through Moylough village with bonfires everywhere. It was just incredible.

I spotted Tom Clancy, a local farmer with a fork and a bale of straw burning brightly. Such were the celebrations that the whole fork and Tom nearly caught fire. It was that kind of night. It was my first year playing Senior and we had won football's biggest prize. We didn't know what it was like to lose. Many of us had played seven games that championship year, winning 6 with 1 draw. However, 2001 was extra special for me personally. I hadn't a great championship heading into that final and had struggled during the year with injuries. On the Saturday morning, before that final, I was at home with my Dad. He asked me to help him on the farm even though I knew it was more than that. It was a pep talk.

We grabbed a few stakes and a sledgehammer and up the farm we went. 'You haven't played well all year' he said. 'But Galway won't win tomorrow if you don't play well. It's on your shoulders.' And down went the stakes into the ground. No pressure. The first half didn't go well the following day, but everything fell into place in part two. We were tactically well set up with the likes of Kevin Walsh outstanding that day. I met my father after the game which was just amazing. It's something I'll never forget.

I think the worst day for me was in 2007 when Westmeath beat us in the football championship qualifiers at home in Galway. We had started brightly but we just never got going fully. I was sharing the free taking with Michael Meehan at the time and I missed one in the second half from about 30 yards out which upset me. It was a terrible miss. In the end, we lost the game by a few points and our summer was over. It was a dark day for Galway football and a very hard one to take. It was probably the toughest defeat in my career. I also missed one of my best friend's wedding in Westport that day.

When you're playing you don't fully appreciate the players you're playing with and the time you have. Former Galway goalkeeper Pat Comer said one time 'it's all about history and geography. You have to be born the right time in the right place with the right people.'

I've played with some of the greatest footballers ever not just in Galway but in this country such as Ja Fallon, Michael Donnellan and Tomas Mannion just to name a few.

I could name the whole team. Ray Silke was a wonderful captain. Unfairly criticised at times for not having the skill that others many have had, he certainly was very influential and effective as a leader. He was always hugely positive and would fill you with confidence heading into big matches.

I look back now on my career with fond memories of those two All Ireland victories but like all sportspeople I still feel we should have won more. The defeat to Kerry in 2000 was hard to take because we should have won the first day. I was captain so it would have been nice to win the All Ireland that year. However, I've always said if we won the title that year we wouldn't have won 2001. That defeat really hurt us and so there was serious hunger in the camp to bounce back from that and make up for it twelve months later. I'm delighted to have played for Galway for so long and get away from it pretty much injury free. To win two medals was great and I'll always have that. I hope Galway go on and win more All Ireland's in the years ahead.

My one piece of advice for any player close to retiring or considering retirement is to have a good and honest chat with your manager. Don't wait for them to have a chat with you. Managers have a huge part to play in players retiring so it can be a smooth landing if it's dealt with properly. A lot of players just get dropped either before, during or after a season ends. They disappear and are often left with a bitter taste. Players should be appreciated a bit more in my view. It's also important that you are retiring for the proper reasons. You've no more to give, you now have other important commitments and you know it's the right time.

You should never prolong your stay as it may damage your legacy. All that good stuff you've done over the years can be undone by one really bad performance.

DAMIEN DUFF

Damien Duff is a former professional soccer player. He's been capped 100 times for Ireland.

Duff played for Blackburn Rovers, Chelsea, Newcastle United and Fulham in England. He also played club football in Australia with Melbourne City and here at home with Shamrock Rovers.

He won two English Premiership titles with Chelsea, English League Cup titles with Blackburn Rovers and Chelsea and was a bronze medallist with Ireland at the 1997 World Youth Championships.

He captained Ireland at the European Soccer Championships in 2012.

Damien lives in Dublin with his wife Elaine and two children Woody and Darcy.

"The first time I saw Damien play I felt
I was watching a wizard and a genius with the ball.
Over the following years he confirmed
my initial evaluation was definitely correct"

BRIAN KERR

DAMIEN DUFF

Since I retired from professional football in December 2015, I'm still trying to figure it all out and what I want from life going forward. It does worry me. It also makes me sad that I'll never love something as much as I did with football. I'll never know how lucky I was to play the beautiful game. I just loved playing and adored every minute of it.

I took a few months off after retiring, eating and drinking what I wanted and doing very little as I tried to adjust to life after sport. There were mornings when I'd leave the house in my car only to pull in on the motorway wondering what am I doing or where was I going.

I'm involved with Shamrock Rovers now in a coaching capacity but it's not the same. The coaching side of things doesn't give me the same buzz as playing. I certainly don't jump out of bed in the morning. I've just found the transition very difficult at times. I've been doing all the UEFA badges, etc but at the minute that's more to keep myself busy. I'm also working with RTÉ Sport as a pundit and enjoying it, but it can be very nerve-wrecking at times. When the red light goes on and the opening music starts playing you know there's no turning back. You're on and you're LIVE. I enjoy the week leading up to the show as I'm preparing and reading up on stuff. I'm also putting my pre-match analysis clips together. It's the closest I've got to what I had on the pitch, the adrenalin rush, the pressure, etc. It will never come close to playing obviously. And then once the show is over it's back to coaching.

There's such a big difference between playing and coaching. As a player, you just look after yourself. As a coach, you are looking after twenty plus footballers. And then there are days when players don't apply themselves properly at training and are not giving it everything. That just makes me so angry and disgusts me. I just find it hard to understand why someone wouldn't want to give their whole heart to football every day.

It's such a massive change to go from playing and doing something you love every day to retiring. There are so many differences. I'd always have an early night if I was training the next day because I always wanted to be the best in training whereas now I just go to bed and don't think too much about the following day.

As a player, every minute of every day was about the match at the weekend. That's all gone now. I don't miss being recognised in the street or people chanting my name. I miss the pure focus and that drive you have as a professional footballer. You want to be the best and beat the best. A lot of ex-players say they miss the banter and miss the craic in the dressing room but to some extent I have that with the coaching staff at Shamrock Rovers. Stephen Bradley, Glenn Cronin and Stephen McPhail are all here, along with Robbie Keane. It's probably my favourite part of the day coming in and chatting with those lads before training starts. That's my dressing room kick now. I miss the lead up to games, working hard, feeling good and looking forward to playing. When you're a sportsperson at that level you feel invincible. You're an elite professional and feel untouchable to some extent. It's the most alive you'll ever feel in your life. It's just a great place to be mentally and physically.

Unless something magical happens, I know I'll never feel that alive again which makes me sad. How will I ever replace playing football? Is there something else out there? Perhaps I think too much about it. I'd just love to feel that alive again so it's just a case of searching for something to replace it. I do get a buzz out of coaching but it's not playing football. Some days I love it, some days I hate it. I'm not going to give up on what might be out there for me, maybe something totally leftfield, etc. At the moment, I'm definitely struggling to find it.

I always knew retirement would come knocking on my door someday but when you're a footballer you just think you're invincible. You don't think about life after sport. Some players hitting thirty start multi-tasking. They start doing their badges or start a degree and that's fine. But for me it was all about playing football. I didn't want to waste an afternoon learning something else.

In my head, I would deal with retirement when it happened. It was a real case of having the blinkers on.

I made up my mind I was retiring from football at the end of October 2015. After recovering from injury, I was on a new contract with Shamrock Rovers but I wasn't enjoying it.

I found myself going to places like Limerick to play a match, only getting a few minutes on the pitch and sometimes not getting on at all. It just sucked the life out of me so I decided that's it, I'm going to retire at the end of the season. It's just time to move on. Not one to make rash decisions I waited until December 2015 to announce it. I wanted to think about my decision but inside I had made up my mind. In the days leading up to it someone drafted a statement for me, I put my own stamp on it and it was sent out. I was so uncomfortable about even issuing a statement about my retirement but I guess that's what you have to do when you're stepping away from the game for the last time.

The news was out that I was retiring and my days as a footballer were over. I thanked my parents and that was it. Christmas was coming and I was looking forward to sharing it with my family. I was now a former professional footballer.

Looking back on my career I still wouldn't be happy. I was never happy at the best of times. I'm probably ultra-hard on myself even to this day whether it's analysing myself on a coaching session or appearing on television. All sportspeople have good and bad days. I had three horrific years up in Newcastle, which I found extremely difficult personally. I got a lot of shit up there but I still wouldn't change that because I think you learn more and improve as a person from the bad times rather than the good. I do anyways. It definitely made me a stronger human being and probably improved me as a footballer too. I know I had ability and worked tirelessly at being a better footballer.

As a footballer, there are moments on the pitch during your career that give you great satisfaction. At home that night again there's a flash of excitement watching it back on Match of the Day. But the next day it's back to work. I was never one to get too carried away. In fact, the older I got the more football turned into a job for me.

When you're eighteen or nineteen you're still on the street - if you know what I mean but as you get older you think about things more seriously and adult like. Indeed, that's something from my career I regret, that as I got older I lost that kid on the street thing probably because of coaching, pressures of the game, money, etc. I think a lot of players lose it which is regretful.

I enjoyed winning trophies, etc. There were good times but it's the more personal moments that stand out for me.

I scored my first premiership goal against Everton with my dad in the crowd alongside a good friend of ours who's sadly passed away. That was a special day.

And then there was a moment in Melbourne I'll never forget. I was lucky enough to walk out with one of my kids beside me who was a mascot at the Melbourne versus Sydney game. That was just brilliant. At that moment, I felt the proudest man on earth. I'd played against Barcelona in the Champions League in front of a packed house on one of the biggest stages in football but give me walking out in front of eight thousand people in Melbourne holding my son's hand any day. It beats the Nou Camp, playing for Ireland or winning trophies. At the end of the day, he's my flesh and blood.

In every sport, there are dark days too. But I've always believed that if you get knocked down you get back up again. Like my days at Newcastle. I also hated the whole celebrity thing around football and found it hard to cope with the attention we all got following the 2002 World Cup in Japan/South Korea. It was just crazy. You couldn't walk down the street, you couldn't even go for a pint in peace. I remember breaking down one night with my mates and saying I just don't like this. I just wanted to go home and close the door. I think it's a very different world now. A lot of young footballers chase the bit I didn't like, going out getting noticed, going to night clubs, having photographs and selfies taken. I just liked playing football and going home.

I still love getting out and kicking a ball. If there's an injury at training I love getting stuck in and running past some of the younger lads. I know I'm lucky at what I've been given. I've a healthy family in my wife Elaine and children Woody and Darcy. It's part two of my life now.

I like the challenge of finding calmness and contentment in my life again and having a reason to properly jump out of bed in the morning.

I'm enjoying the coaching side of things but don't see myself managing in Ireland. Maybe Australia or America but who knows. My kids are my boss now so if they don't want to go then we'll be staying here in Ireland. I would never mess with my children's education, their friends here, etc.

When it comes to retirement I think everybody is different. I know plenty of sportspeople who had a plan heading towards their thirties. I didn't but I wouldn't change the way I did it.

If someone was thinking about retiring I'm a big believer in walking before you're asked to walk. I could have squeezed a bit more out of playing with Ireland but I'm a proud man and wouldn't have enjoyed being on the bench. I wouldn't have been able to handle that so it was about getting the timing right which is a skill in its own. I think a lot of people maybe go on for too long. When I retired even if I felt I had made the wrong decision I would have stuck with it. I remember when Shay [Given] came back out of retirement I remember thinking I wouldn't do that. But everybody is different. I knew it was the right time for me to go. The problem is many sportspeople fight that and end up being dropped or let go.

VALERIE MULCAHY

Valerie Mulcahy from Cork is regarded as one of the greatest ever ladies footballers to play the game.

After playing at the highest level for nearly 15 years Valerie retired from football in April 2016. Throughout her career she won an incredible 31 Senior titles with her county including 10 All Ireland Senior medals.

She wore the Cork jersey for the final time in September 2015 when the rebels beat Dublin by two points in Croke Park.

She's also been named All Ireland Final player of the match on three occasions.

In 2015, she became the first high profile ladies GAA star to speak publicly about being gay. In June of that year she married long term girlfriend Meg Blyth.

Valerie is an executive member of the Women's Gaelic Players' Association.

"The complete package – incredible skill, complemented by an exceptional work ethic and an unflappable temperament"

EAMONN RYAN

VALERIE MULCAHY

I had to prepare myself for retirement. It was a difficult decision. If sport is an addiction, then retiring is like coming down off something. When you have something in your life for so long, it's hard to live without it. You have to be able to cope without it and be content with your decision, particularly if it's something that's given you a lot of satisfaction for a very long time. You no longer have that structure in your life. There's no more training, no more travelling and you're no longer competing at the highest level. As well as that, a huge amount of your identity has been wrapped up in the sport for years. You now have a new identity.

I had to be mentally ok with the decision to retire and be ready for life after sport. So much of your happiness can be caught up in your sport, so it's important to prepare yourself and have other outlets. So, I took up some new hobbies and started doing other things before I retired which really helped. I play a bit of soccer now which keeps me fit and keeps that competitiveness that will always be in me. I also get to travel abroad a lot more now, something I could never really do while playing competitive sport for nearly 15 years. I love to travel.

It takes a bit of adjusting and time to get used to retirement. A lot of players who retired before me said they still miss the big day, that buzz and how much they would look forward to playing and competing. When that goes, it's very hard to replace it. I do think players struggle with life after sport but the extent to which they do depends on the person, it depends on why they had to retire or when they had to retire, whether it was an injury or if they were not involved as much as they would like to be.

I was lucky I retired on my own terms. I would have found it very hard not to be playing every minute of every game. I was extremely fortunate in that I started and finished the majority of games in my career. Over time, I just got used to that and never really learned how to cope with the anxiety of the game from the side line.

I would have either really struggled with that or have had to learn how to process that if I had continued to play as I got older.

Apart from my new hobbies and playing some soccer, I started doing some media work with TG4 and RTÉ after I retired which helped fill my time and feed my interest. It means I still get to go the games, which keeps me distracted and occupied in one way and fulfilled in another. I went to the 2016 All Ireland Ladies Senior Football Final and I was able to enjoy it as an analyst whereas if I was up in the stand and there as a supporter I would have been so anxious because it was my first year as a non player. I would have been trying to kick every ball and asking myself why I wasn't down there togged out and playing.

There was a moment in 2015 when I decided that's it, it's time to retire. I had been considering for a long time how and when I should retire and I had been appreciating much more than usual all the success we had experienced as a team over the years. I had just gotten married and my mother in law was terminally ill. Life outside football was getting bigger and fuller for me and others were becoming more reliant on me, so spending so much time on football was getting harder to justify to myself.

We were playing in the quarter final of the championship against Galway, and I had been playing well all year, but got taken off early in the second half. I found it so difficult to come off and not be able to contribute and was just so frustrated that I couldn't be out there doing something to help win it. For the first time in my life, I started thinking about retirement and questioning whether I would be a very good team mate if I wasn't actually playing.

In the end, we went on to win another All Ireland and my 10th medal in all but at that stage I had begun to see my playing career not just in the now but as a whole, from the start to the potential end and I wanted the bigger picture to have the best possible ending.

In the following weeks, I met up with some people who know me and would know my sporting abilities and limitations, and indeed people I trusted and mentioned the word retirement to them. My uncle would have been one of them. He basically said 'you've had a great career and you're right to go now.' He just reaffirmed what I thought myself and what my closest friends and family were reiterating to me.

At the start of every season, every player thinks about what's ahead of them and all that's involved in the year. The travelling, the training, all those weekends away and everything and everyone you will miss. It is a massive commitment and not easy to balance everything including work, life and now marriage for me.

My wife had followed me to every end of the country and had supported me in every way possible since I have known her. Now her own mother was sick and I wanted to be available to support her as she had supported me.

I've always been very competitive and certainly miss that. I also miss training, which was very competitive too. I miss the crack, the banter, the friendships and been part of something great. We still meet up but not as much as three and four times a week when you're playing. I miss the buzz and all that comes with the big games. I miss playing in Croke Park.

What I don't miss is the worry that was attached to playing for me. As a forward and as the primary free taker, I felt hugely responsible for our scoring and although I practiced as much as I could through my career, it didn't always stop me worrying about making mistakes or console me when I did make them. I had to work a lot on trusting myself and accepting the misses and slip ups when they happened.

I really enjoyed my final game in Croke Park. I knew I was about to retire and that it would be my last game. I just savored the moment. I wasn't looking back or looking forward. I was just living in the present.

It was such a great feeling. I also knew I was in a very fortunate position. I was leaving the sport I love on my own terms. That was hugely important to me.

A lot of sportspeople don't get that choice and find it incredibly difficult to deal with after they retire from sport. I was also leaving at a great time. We had won another All Ireland title with an incredible team and I played my part.

I was very content with my decision to retire. For 15 years, I had prioritised ladies football over everything else in my life. I look back on my career with so many wonderful memories. There were so many great days and magical moments.

One of those days, my most treasured day in my career, has to be the 2014 All Ireland Senior Football Final against Dublin. We were being well beaten and for the first time ever, it looked like we would be beaten in Croke Park. Thankfully, we managed to produce a very memorable comeback that I will be proud of for the rest of my life. That win, that moment gave me great joy and still brings a smile to my face every time I think about it. I think that final alone really heightened everybody's awareness of ladies football around country. There was also a massive television audience that day.

Winning is an amazing feeling. I kind of feel there are two types of winning. There's winning when you're the underdog and that incredible feeling of victory and jubilation at the final whistle. And then there's winning when you're expected to win and it's just become the norm and just pure relief of defending your position. You're just so happy you've managed not to lose.

Losing can be a complete shock and it can hurt, really hurt. We lost the 2010 All Ireland Senior Football Quarter Final to Tyrone after being well up at half time. The reality that we'd lost was shocking. I didn't cry that day. In a funny way, I always knew that day would come and it's a horrible place to be. It was so disappointing and I didn't know what to do for the rest of the season.

Thankfully, I've been very lucky as a player and the great team I've played with that I haven't experienced loss too often, for which I am so grateful to my coach and my team mates. I've always enjoyed that winning feeling and always loved playing in Croke Park. I got to play there for the first time in 2005 after we beat Mayo in the Semi-Final. For so long we had watched other teams play there, year after year, so it was a dream come true that's for sure. Before that it was just a pipe dream. We had finally made it to an All-Ireland Final and beaten Mayo, the team who had dominated ladies football for so long.

I have been fortunate to have experienced winning Munster titles, All Ireland titles and have been All-Ireland Final Player of the Match on three different occasions so I've enjoyed a very successful career. Nothing will ever replace playing. The buzz, the adrenalin, that winning feeling, it's a drug and it's hard to give it up. I've had the time of my life and have little to complain about.

I help out with the coaching side of things at school now and have being manager of the Interprovincial girls schools team. There is great joy in trying to develop players and watching them enjoy the sport.

Looking back on my career, I'll always been very grateful for everything I have had. I was never arrogant or ungrateful for a minute. We came from such lows having five players at training for a championship match and getting thrashed by Waterford and Kerry in the Munster football championship to achieving greatness in the sport. I never won anything underage with Cork, so that allowed me to be grateful and appreciate the big days we had and take advantage of the times we had together. Having to put in the work without the reward underage helped me to be grateful during my senior career – I appreciated everything we experienced.

It far exceeded anything I ever imagined, hoped or dreamed of. I had a dream of winning one All Ireland. We won 10 with an unbelievable team. It was amazing to be part of something great. We made history, we changed the record books and helped increase the profile of ladies football in the process. I got to travel to some amazing places in the world on All Star trips.

I am deeply honoured that people consider me one of the greatest players. I met so many great people who helped, guided and supported me along the way.

Summer will never be the same without my Cork jersey and football boots, as I know I'll never have those special moments again. So, it's hugely important for sportspeople to enjoy every moment particularly as you get older and your career is coming to an end. My advice to players now is to be present, enjoy the moment for what it is and savour the journey.

EOIN KELLY

Eoin Kelly retired from inter-county hurling in December 2014. He won 2 All Ireland Senior Hurling medals with Tipperary, including captaining his county to the title in 2010 when they beat Kilkenny.

He won his first All-Ireland Senior Hurling medal in 2001 when Tipperary beat Galway in the final. Kelly also picked up a National League medal, a Munster Senior Hurling medal and the young hurler of the year award that year.

Throughout his career, he scored 21 goals and 368 points which makes him one of the highest championship scorers of all time. He made 63 championship appearances for his county before retiring from the inter-county scene.

Kelly is regarded as one of the greatest hurlers ever to wear the blue and gold winning six All Star awards during his career.

Eoin lives in Tipperary with his wife Sarah and children Conal, Eve and Rory.

96

"Eoin was an outstanding leader who always performed when it mattered most**"**

LIAM SHEEDY

EOIN KELLY

It was January 1st, 2014 and the alarm clock was ringing. It was 8am and just hours after a typical mad Irish wedding. I was best man to former Clare hurler, Barry Nugent.

I was lying in bed in Spanish Point, County Clare and due at the Horse & Jockey in Tipperary for a pre-season meeting at 10am followed by training at noon. I turned to my wife Sarah and said "What am I doing? I don't think I'm going to go back to this" as the clock ticked on. It was now 8.40am. In the end, I went. I made the meeting and performed well in training which included 8 x 400 metre runs. Management were happy with what they'd seen and I made it very clear to everybody that I wasn't going anywhere. I gave it everything that year, but when I didn't get any game time, I knew my career was as good as over. It was very frustrating.

In December 2014, I announced I was retiring from the county scene and there was no turning back.

I think everyone's retirement can be different, so I can only describe my own retirement. For the first 12 months I was able to fill that void. I was busy with both work and home life, while doing some punditry on the radio. So, I was going to the Tipperary games not like your normal supporter. I felt protected as I had my media pass to get me in to the ground. I was up in the commentary box doing analysis, discussing the game so my mind was occupied. There was a buzz about it. I felt I was on my own watching the game. I suppose I was somewhat afraid to be in the stand watching games, people asking what you think, meeting other players...

Being a pundit, I also enjoyed watching other things from the commentary box, like what was going on pitch side, how teams were setting up, wondering what was going through the manager's mind, etc.

Being involved in the media that first year certainly helped with retirement. I still felt very much part of the game. It was like a soft landing.

Apart from the media work, Rory my youngest was born, I was building a new house and I was studying for exams. Bank exams I'd put off while training and playing for Tipperary.

To be honest, I tried to get away from the GAA. I'd gone back training with the club in early January 2015 but I had put on a few pounds [I had a tendency to do that over the years] and my back was giving me trouble so I really felt I wasn't up for it and played little or no part. However, I did miss it and come the summer the club pulled me back in again despite not being in great physical shape. I played in goals [the local butcher and first choice goalkeeper wasn't available] and I was back playing. However, I remember pucking out the ball [late in the game] and my back was killing me. I just wasn't enjoying it and was struggling. But I kept going and continued playing for the club in 2015. I played outfield in the local Semi-Final scoring 5 points from play and I was delighted with my contribution. Despite not being in great shape, my experience, cuteness and ability got me through. However, I knew myself it was a big drawback to have missed the Winter training and pre-season conditioning earlier in the year. I promised myself that it wouldn't happen in 2016.

So, what did I miss must from playing with the county? I missed being physically fit from training and playing at the highest level. You just felt so good. I always enjoyed training and liked to be in Thurles early. It was great to get out of the suit and throw on the gear. I was relaxed and ready for another Tipperary training session, which was always tough, tense and demanding.

I always found the club games so much easier. You'd shift a club player handy enough because they mightn't have the work done you'd have done. You'd feel you could dominate a club game.

When I retired from playing with the county, I missed that high intensity of everything. The big match days, meeting in the Horse & Jockey before the game, the calmness at lunch before everything got very serious. Once that team meeting started after lunch everyone was well and truly tuned in. There was total silence. The management spoke and we were ready.

I felt involved in something special and I was in that zone that all players want to be in ahead of an important game. At the end of the day, only thirty lads are chosen and you are one of the thirty. I always wanted to be in the starting fifteen, but when I was finishing up, I was number seventeen or eighteen. I always wanted to play. So much so that you'd nearly be hoping that someone was carrying an injury [not in a bad minded way] and that you'd get the call up to replace him. I was always hoping, always anxious, always wanting to be in the middle of it and that's just normal for a typical sportsman. You'd be buzzing after training, after the big games, after the emotive team talks. You'd find yourself driving faster, moving quicker and doing things at a higher intensity. Those are some of the biggest things I really miss.

My last game with Tipperary was the 2014 All Ireland Senior Hurling Final drawn game against Kilkenny. That year, we got to the Allianz League Final losing out again to Brian Cody's men and I didn't get any game time. I just felt I wasn't in Tipperary management's plans. I didn't play any part in the championship game against Limerick. Indeed, I played very little that year. But something kept me going all season and I stuck it out. Imagine if we won, imagine having my son Conal with me on the day and the pictures that would follow. Conal, Liam McCarthy and me. As it worked out I got the picture but minus Liam. I knew that was it for me after the All Ireland Hurling Final replay. I wouldn't play in Croke Park again.

To be honest I remember coming out of the stadium after that game feeling very low and bitterly disappointed. It was a quiet bus. We had just lost another final. You know what's ahead of you for the next 24 hours: Lots of post-match analysis and post mortems. And then there's the homecoming. I remember Sarah sat beside me and we said to each other "this is the last time". However, it's still not real for those 24 hours because you're with the team and lads you would die for on the pitch.

The following morning [the replay was played on the Saturday] we [Sarah, John O'Brien and his wife Siobhan and a few other players] slipped away for some quiet time and pretty much acknowledged the fact that it was over for us.

And that was it.

Looking back now, I really miss being involved in that competitive environment where the intensity levels and stakes are so high. I loved winning. After 2010 I felt different, I was in a different headspace, had a different mentality. I think being involved in that kind of winning environment really develops you as a person both mentally and physically. You're a better person for it. That's probably what I miss most.

As a Tipperary Senior hurler for over fifteen years, I've experienced plenty of highs and lows.

My greatest day in a Tipperary jersey was in 2006. It was a day that everything went right for me. I felt so free that day. It was against Limerick in the Munster hurling championship. I scored 14 points that day [nine from play]. Limerick hit us with two early goals and we were chasing the game. Instead of being rocked I just felt let's go at it, let's see what happens, I don't care. I felt so free. You might hit two or three of them days in your life. Everything just went according to plan for the rest of that game. That was my best day in the blue and gold. It's a day you'd just love to experience again and again. We beat the old enemy and neighbours Limerick. I was twenty-four at the time but I felt like I was twelve pucking the ball off the wall at home pretending to be John Leahy or Nicky English.

I've seen winning dressing room's both as a young nineteen-year-old and as an experienced leader. At nineteen, it's all new to you, you're a bit quiet. 2001 and the All Ireland victory over Galway in the final is still a bit of a blur. I was so young. I was thinking is that it, sure this will happen again next year and a few years after. But of course that didn't happen.

The Liam McCarthy cup in 2001 was presented on the pitch that day which was unusual [the Hogan Stand was being re-built so wasn't available] and as a young boy growing up in Tipperary I always wanted to climb the steps of the Hogan and lift hurling's biggest prize. Thankfully, that dream did come true nine years later in 2010. I respected and understood it so much more that year and found it so much more different to 2001. Yes, I did have a big role as a nineteen-year-old nine years earlier taking the frees, but I still felt like a periphery player. Where as in 2010 when I was captain, the dressing room felt very different this time. I really felt I'd made an impact in making the ecstasy that was in the room. I really felt like one of the guys who had created this bliss.

The difference between winning and losing is huge.

I remember 2009, Tipperary selector Eamon O 'Shea thrown down and grieving after the defeat. Losing any game is tough. Losing an All-Ireland is heart breaking. On the flip side I loved seeing the joy on other people's faces when we won, especially the All Ireland's, that's probably the biggest enjoyment, the biggest satisfaction I got from those days.

That couple of minutes in the dressing room after victory is special. Lads just let themselves go, they just throw off the shackles and they're dancing and jumping around the room. Everything that's inside them just comes out, especially the quieter lads. That feeling you've done it, that moment.

I've a picture of my Dad with the Liam McCarthy Cup in the dressing room after we won the All Ireland title in 2010. I picked it up recently and just thought thank God. I know how proud he was because he is a big GAA man. I loved the joy he got from watching Tipperary, from watching his son's play, sitting in the kitchen at home, chatting about the game and previewing the next one.

I'd say they were more disappointed when I retired than I was because they would have enjoyed me playing on. It kept them and the home house alive.

I've been in a few losing dressing rooms as well throughout the years and it's like being at a funeral and in a morgue. It's like a family member has died. That's what it is. You're afraid to do anything, afraid to stick your head up in case someone makes eye contact with you.

You're afraid to be the first one to go into the shower because lads might start talking about you, you're just numb. It's so quiet. Everything is heard. If you tip toe out to the toilet you're heard even if you're just in your socks. You don't want to be the first to make that move, you just want to grieve. You are grieving. My toughest day, most painful day was the 2009 All Ireland Hurling Final and that defeat to Kilkenny. I played well that day but I beat myself up badly over a goal chance I missed. We should and could have scored a lot more that day but didn't. Kilkenny hit a purple patch in the second half and punished us. We hurled very well so when that happens in sport, defeat is even harder to accept. There was a point in that game when we were three points up [middle of second half] and I felt we weren't going to be beaten. We really believed in ourselves and everything was going well until the closing stages. It was our first final since 2001 and we really wanted it. Sadly, we lost and it was devastating. The dressing room was horrible, the bus was horrible and going into the Burlington Hotel was the worst as you met your family and friends. There were lots of tears. Anytime you lose you just feel you've let the people down, those you love, those you care about, the supporters, the management, etc. I felt I'd let them all down. It's terrible, it's an awful feeling.

I suppose they are days when I look back on my career and wish I had achieved more. Those barren years when you weren't even on the radar are a bit of a regret. You'd love to have them again but I guess you can only control the controllable. Playing hurling for your county is a journey. It's a wonderful journey that takes you to great places.

You get to meet great people, you meet people who face huge challenges on a daily basis, people not so fortunate who love Tipperary more than life and just love going to matches and supporting the team. I always loved meeting those people and seeing the joy they got from talking about the game and taking photographs, etc.

It meant the world to them. But it also meant the world to me. It kept me humble and appreciate what I had and what I was bringing to the table. I'd like to think I kept my feet on the ground.

Like all players, I always worried about getting injured. Any player is just one bad injury away from being a vulnerable character and missing out on playing. I was lucky.

THE PSYCHOLOGY OF RETIRING
NIAMH FITZPATRICK

I've been working as a psychologist since 1991. The reason I became a psychologist was because I had problems in sport myself. From the age of ten, I was hugely involved in equestrian sport; I did show-jumping and eventing. I really enjoyed representing my club, school and later university. It became apparent that I was relatively good at the initial stages but as soon as I got to a final and my coach would say 'I need a good clear fast round from you' I'd panic and lose my way. I just didn't have the psychological tools to back up the bit of talent I had in the sport. I felt like I was no good at it and that's just the way it was for me, that there was nothing that could be done about it.

I had wanted to do Law when I left school and I missed out on the points by the narrowest of margins and so pursued an Arts Degree at UCD, with the plan to go in to Law via the back door. I chose psychology as one of my subjects. I completely fell in love with it and in the course of my studies I found a field within psychology devoted to teaching people how to prepare mentally for sport. I realised then that I wasn't poor at my own sport, it was just a case of not having had the psychological skillset to access that talent when under pressure. After graduating, I did a Masters in Clinical Psychology [UCD] followed by a MSc specialising in Sport Psychology [United States Sports Academy]. Part of this was an internship which actually allowed me to follow an Olympic psychologist in London for twelve months. It was an incredible experience and I learned so much. Today, I work with people from a variety of sports, a lot of GAA players as well as athletes preparing for all levels of events from the Olympic Games to local competitions. I help them with their mental preparation, so that when under pressure they can access the talent that they have. I also work with people outside of sport who may be experiencing anxiety, depression or stress.

In addition, I work with both teams and individuals from the corporate world seeking to achieve optimum performance in their field. I love my job, it is what I was born to do.

I love sport and have worked with some great people and teams over the years. One team that stands out in my mind is Liam Griffin and the Wexford Senior Hurling team. I still remember to this day, the colour, excitement and noise of September 1st 1996 when Wexford beat Limerick in the All Ireland Hurling Final. It was just incredible, seeing this band of men achieve what they set out to achieve, having overcome both internal and external obstacles along the way.

Life after sport and that transition from playing sport to retiring is huge. I compare it to parents when a child leaves home and the empty nest syndrome kicks in. Or a child moving from a primary school into a new secondary school without their friends. We tend to struggle with any significant shift in our lives or any movement to a different phase.

One reason that retirement from sport can be so challenging is because there's an identity attached to that previous phase. Athletes eat, sleep and drink their sport so when it's over it can be hugely challenging. A common feeling is "what am I now if I'm not an athlete?"

Secondly, the support structure disappears. When they retire as a competitor, the athlete no longer has a team around them; guiding them, supporting them, believing in them, people who are there during the good times and the bad. Suddenly there's nobody around. Retiring from work is quite similar as we no longer have colleagues, a manager, a support structure around, that support network is gone. This can be hugely challenging and can feel quite isolating.

Related to that can be the camaraderie that often goes hand in hand with participation in sports. Competitors spend so much time with teammates or coaching staff, often more time than they spend with their families. Bonds develop as people begin to work together towards a shared goal.

Trust, honesty, support can cement those bonds. So, what happens when an athlete retires from sport and finds themselves without these friendships? It can feel lonely, often like a loss.

Also, athletes have been training three, four, five times a week for the last twenty years or so and suddenly they no longer have to train. So, what do they do with all the energy that was invested in sport, a sport that no longer plays a pivotal role in their world?

Yet that energy, that drive, that need to push, to achieve, to succeed is still there. What do they do with all those feelings?

I've seen athletes suffer with huge levels of stress, with anxiety and depression as well as feelings of isolation after they retire from sport. They are just lost and that can take its toll on an athlete mentally. They have been so used to feeling in control, to feeling strong even in the face of adversity, to feeling like they are the master of their own destiny, and now they can feel vulnerable They've been so used to trying and failing and learning. That's the cycle in sport. Now they face an open space in front of them and they've nothing. Not even that cycle of trying and failing. Therefore, if somebody is not prepared for life after sport, if they're not supported through the transition or don't have plans around it they'll quickly find a huge amount of space for the mind. And the mind will fill that space. This can be dangerous for athletes if not managed well, as it can spiral into a downward cycle. "Did I achieve my goals?" "Did I retire too early?" "Was it worth all those sacrifices that I made in my life for sport or did I waste my life?" "What do I do with my life now?" "Do I matter to anyone anymore?" "Do I contribute?" These are all quite common thoughts and in and of themselves they are not a problem, but, if not managed they can build and in time contribute to a state of depression or anxiety.

I was the HQ Sport Psychologist with the Irish team for three Olympic Games: Athens 2004, Beijing 2008 and London 2012 and I'm currently working with the Irish eventing team ahead of Tokyo 2020.

The Olympics is interesting in that when you see an athlete going into what is probably their last Olympics and you know they don't have a family, they don't have work or studies to go to after they finish, and they will be retiring from their sport after this Games, then for us as a medical and sports science team it's a red flag.

Because having nothing else in their life puts so much pressure on that Games performance and it also provides a petri dish for after the Olympics in which anxiety and depression can grow very nicely. It's just so important such an athlete is hugely prepared and supported before and after competition and not just during.

There are two keys things to seriously consider when retiring from sport. Firstly, what are you retiring to? And secondly, have you a preparation plan in place to deal with that retirement process? Personally, I haven't seen a massive difference between amateur and professional sportspeople retiring from sport.

I find the biggest differences are in the person themselves, be it their character, personality or their psychological tool set. Some are better set up to deal with the change in their life than others but whether you're an amateur or professional athlete you still must deal with life after sport at some point.

The first thing I do in helping athletes deal with life after sport is that I bring the topic up. Most if not all athletes don't really think about the future. Yes, they plan for their sport but their plans always come back to the present. They are quite present focused which they need to be in order to get the very best out of their performance. A good analogy is a bride and groom getting married. It's all about the wedding, the planning and the preparation. But what about the marriage and the future? Isn't that important too? The bit about what comes after the wedding day? I sit down with an athlete and look at their whole life. Who are the people in their life? What are the demands on them? What are their interests? I'm looking to see if there's balance in their life or if it's a situation where sport is their whole life and they've nothing else. I would then discuss their options, their education, their strengths and resources. We look at what they'd like to do now that their sports career is coming to an end. I try and bring them from a plan that is sometimes vague into an action that is more specific. It's basically preparing them for the Monday after they retire from sport on Sunday and that feeling of emptiness, loneliness and isolation that may be present.

The Irish Institute of Sport is a great resource in terms of programmes to guide athletes through this transition out of sport and into a new chapter in their life, so I might guide someone in that direction as well as doing some work with them myself.

There isn't a right or wrong way of dealing with life after sport. There's certainly no rule book. However, it is important to realise that while you had an amazing life in sport you can have a beautiful and challenging life after sport. It's just a case of turning the page to the next chapter. Athletes tend to look back on their careers and at what they lost rather than what they won. I try to help them open their eyes, to widen their perspective and get them to see what they achieved, both in terms of results and trophies but also in terms of what they collected along the way in terms of skills, qualities and resources. I also get them to look at what they might gain or what they could experience in the future – not only focusing on the loss, also seeing the possible gains. For example, it could be that somebody who enjoyed a great career in sport as a player goes on to have a great career in management of a sporting team.

However, it is important to give yourself enough time mentally to accept that you're no longer an athlete before you start doing your badges or take up a management role, etc. I've seen retired players step into a coaching role but they're not really there as a coach. They're there as a coach who still wants to be an athlete. They look at the athletes on the field not through the objective eyes that they should do, but through their own eyes. In this case they are less effective as a coach.

It's hugely important to have support from your family and friends when you retire. You might be a hurler or footballer but at the end of the day you are a person first. You are a mother, father, son or daughter, brother or sister. There's nothing wrong in asking your family for support, as life after sport can be a frightening place at times. For years, your family has been the sports team that you've played with, trained with, travelled with, they're a second family in many respects. However, now that your career is over you've returned to your first family and it's important that they understand the challenges in dealing with life after sport.

If you're thinking about retiring or on the verge of retiring, start by looking at your interests. Our attention follows our interest. To go from something that got you, grabbed you and that you loved so much to having something you just endure is not ok for anybody in life. So, start by thinking what interests you and do not compare that to your sport because at first you're not going to find something you love as much as that sport. Also, what are the options available to you? Should you go and talk to somebody about this, such a psychologist, coach, or parent? As a player, you put as much effort as you could into training your mind, your body and your skillset. Doesn't it make sense to put that same effort into looking at life after sport? Talking to someone else will help you see what you can't see yourself. It's a second pair of eyes. They will help you look at your options, your interests, your identity and life after sport.

I think the conversation is only beginning to happen now about life after sport. There simply isn't enough awareness about it despite best efforts to get it out there. This is because what's exciting, what makes headlines, what's interesting for people is the now, the battle, the highs and the lows of competitive sport. Going back to a 'normal' life just doesn't sound as exciting, but it absolutely can be.

The more we talk about retirement from sport and the challenges faced within, and the more that's written about it the better. It will lead to a better understanding of an athlete's career and life after sport and this will bring us to being better able to support these athletes when they do prepare to hang up the sports shoes for good.

KENNY EGAN

Kenny Egan is a former Irish boxer who won a silver medal at the 2008 Olympic Games in Beijing.

He also won two European Amateur Championship bronze medals in 2006 and 2010 and an incredible 10 National Senior titles.

He now works as an addiction counsellor and as a Fine Gael councillor in South Dublin.

Kenny lives in Dublin with his wife Karen, their daughter Kate and Karen's daughter Kelis.

"Kenny's judgement of distance and his perfect timing made him stand out head and shoulders above the rest"

BILLY WALSH

KENNY EGAN

I retired in 2013 but there have been times since then that I've thought about coming back and returning to the ring. In the initial stages of retirement, I felt I was still fit enough, I could go back into camp and make a comeback. There is also an element of regret that I didn't go professional looking at a lot of the Irish boxers now, such as Michael Conlon, who are doing so well. If I had spearheaded that back in 2010 then who knows, but I just wasn't in the right frame of mind at the time. I made a decision to remain amateur until 2012 and try my best to get to London, but sadly that didn't happen. At that stage, I had enough travelling around the world, competing, trying to make my weight and not really getting on with life. I was pushing thirty and I felt I had nothing to show for it. Yes, I had an Olympic silver medal but you can't walk into a bank with a medal and say you're looking for a mortgage. It was a massive dose of reality when I did retire in 2013.

At the beginning, I was blaming the IABA for not hiring me as a coach but it was my own fault. I had no education. In hindsight, I should have been studying while I was competing but that never entered my mind. I was just so focused on being the best, winning an Olympic medal and fulfilling my dreams. I had no time for study. I now encourage all young athletes to study while training and competing. There are certainly no guarantees in sport. The reality is that you might not win an Olympic medal, you mightn't even qualify for an Olympic Games. You could end up with nothing. There are so many boxers I know who got beaten in National finals and just disappeared. That was it, it was over. I was lucky. I won titles. I won an Olympic medal.

I remember my last fight, losing to Joe Ward at the National Stadium in February, 2013. He was better than me and I admit that. He was hungrier and an exceptional talent. There was a great atmosphere in the stadium that night, but I was beaten fair and square and knew that was it for me. I had enough of boxing and walked back to my corner to tell my coaches.

After that, I went back into the centre of the ring, took the microphone from the master of ceremonies and announced my retirement.

Everybody stood up and applauded. There were people there who weren't old enough to see me win my first National title. It was nice too because it was a full house and the place I'd won my first National title back in 2001. Thirteen finals later, the show was finally over and I was handing over the mantle to a young boxer with great talent in Joe Ward. I woke up the following morning knowing that I was now a former boxer. It was the end of one chapter and the start of another. But what would I do now? All I knew was boxing.

After I retired in 2013, I found it very difficult to fill the void. Boxing had been my life, it was all I knew and all I ever wanted to do. I continued to train which included running, sparring and bag work. I really wanted to maintain my fitness and my shape. Body image is such a big factor for athletes when they retire because they are so used to looking fit and healthy. It can be difficult looking in the mirror a couple of months after you retire and asking what have I done to myself? There's low self-esteem, low self-worth and often hate. I'm now 20kg heavier than when I fought so it's important I keep moving and eating well. However, life is busy now. I have a wife, a family, I'm a local councillor in the area and now a qualified counsellor. I no longer have the luxury of training twice a day, then resting followed by eating and training again. Those days are well and truly over. That's an athlete's life and sadly I'm not an athlete anymore.

Being a local councillor has been very interesting. I enjoy going to meetings, putting in motions, etc. But it's still all very new to me. It's a different type of fighting. Trying to get things done sometimes can be very frustrating in politics. I'm enjoying being a counsellor too and would love to set up my own practice some day or work at the Irish Institute of sport helping athletes. Having that piece of paper finally is so important.

After I retired in 2013, I approached Billy and Zour about working with them and getting involved in coaching. However, there were no vacancies at the time. I waited for a position but nothing arrived. I did a couple of sessions on the house to help out but I knew I was worth more than just a slap on the back after winning an Olympic silver medal.

I told Billy I couldn't hang around and I left. I had to do it. Shortly after that, I started college. The personal development of what I've learnt about myself and where I've come from and where I am now has been amazing.

Even when sportspeople retire and move into good jobs, I still don't think they're happy. You're leaving behind something great, something you've loved doing for so long. It's like a death in your life. Half of me died after Beijing. The drinking, the partying and the madness was just a way of forgetting about the end. When I officially retired in 2013, half of me said thank god because that was it now. Boxing was no more. All athletes will tell you we don't think about retirement until it's staring us right in the face. A high-performance athlete at twenty-six is at a slippery slope to retirement. That's the world of sport. You are in and out very quickly. Planning is the key to retiring. It's going to come at some stage for every athlete across every sport. You don't think about it when you're in the mist of playing and competing for the big prizes. Everybody is patting you on the back and there is no talk of such thing.

However, the clock keeps ticking unfortunately for all of us and you do have to hang up the gloves at some stage.

I always wanted to go to the Olympic Games and win a medal. I didn't qualify for Athens in 2004 and was bitterly disappointed. I had no choice but to pick myself up and give it another four years and do everything in my power to qualify for Beijing in 2008. I did and went on to win a silver medal at the Games. It was brilliant but having nothing to fall back on was frightening. When the bell rang at the end of the 2008 Olympic boxing final I wasn't thinking this is unbelievable, my life will change forever, I'm an Olympic silver medallist, the world is my oyster. I was just thinking what the fuck do I do now? I wanted that fight to last forever but, of course, it didn't. As a young boy growing up in Dublin I had watched Michael Carruth win an Olympic Gold medal in Barcelona and 16 years later here I was standing in the ring picking up a silver.

I knew that the chances of making London in 2012 were slim. It would mean another four years of hard training, lots of travelling and unbelievable sacrifices. I certainly considered retirement at the time but I was only twenty-six. I was also receiving good funding [€40,000 a year] along with bonuses, public appearances, etc on the back of my Olympic success. I felt good, I was in great shape and went on to win a bronze medal at the 2010 European Amateur Championships in Moscow. I felt I could make London and so I continued with my training, etc. However, I was drinking a lot after Beijing, partying hard and burning the candle at both ends. I was in a bad place. It always amazes me how stubborn the body is and how much stick it can take and I'm a witness of that. It's an amazing piece of apparatus. Mentally I was destroyed and I knew if I didn't stop I'd end up on the street.

I had visions of me sitting at a bar in twenty years' time, giving some young lad a nudge and pointing at a picture saying that was me winning in Beijing, will you buy me a pint? I just felt so lost after the 2008 Olympics. I know I won medals after that, but 2008 to 2010 is still a blur to this day. I finally stopped drinking in 2010. I probably would have gone professional after Beijing but I was in no mental state to do so. Sportspeople talk about filling the void after they retire but I found it very difficult to fill the void after Beijing.

Today all the medals and achievements mean nothing if I haven't got peace of mind. Thankfully, I'm over the hill now. Yes, there are days when I feel like a drink but I'm a much stronger person now and able to stay clear of it. Your head can certainly get you into trouble at times that's why I think the soul is hugely important. I learnt that while studying.

I finished college in May 2017 with a degree in psychotherapy, which included a thesis on 'Male Olympians retirement from High Performance Sport and Mitigating the Risk.' It looked at what an Olympian is worth and who benefits out of the Olympic Games. In this country, there are no structures in place to help Olympians after they retire. You have no choice but to look after yourself. In my view, I don't think Olympians are appreciated enough in Ireland because we are so rare. Most people think it's just two weeks every four years but it's so much more than that. There are incredible sacrifices. It's a fusion of blood, sweat and tears and qualification. There are people who start boxing late in their life and qualify for a major competition but most start early followed by a relentless pursuit to master the sport and hopefully qualify for an Olympic Games.

The Irish Institute of Sport help athletes who have an interest in education and various different courses. But I think it needs to be mandatory that if you want to be part of an Irish team, then you have to do A, B and C along with your training.

Therefore, you have something to fall back on when you retire from sport. Your talent means little to you when you're looking for a job after you retire from sport. I know a former Irish Olympian who was a super hero in their day but shortly after they retired and went looking for a job nobody wanted to know them. The same Olympian went around handing out over two hundred CVs and got no reply. Everybody knew his name but no one would give him a job. Just how degrading is that. You go from being a National hero to a nobody. Imagine the effect that had on him. Being an Olympian is very special but it's not enough. I don't want to be known for the rest of my life as Kenny Egan, the Olympian. That silver medal is now at home in my mother's house under the bed. I take it out every so often to look at it. It will always be there but that's not going to feed my family and that scares me.

In my view I think every Olympic medallist in this country should be automatically put on a state pension once you retire from sport. It would give athletes such a huge incentive to win a medal along with a massive sense of security after they finish. It certainly wouldn't break the bank.

My greatest day was in April 2008 in Athens. It was my sixth attempt at qualifying for an Olympics. I had tried on three different occasions in 2004 but had failed to qualify for the Games.

I'd already tried twice to qualify for Beijing but had come up short each time. So, it was make or break time. I was fighting a German boxer and it was two all after the first round. Time stood still as I got up for the remainder of the fight. Could I finally qualify for an Olympic Games or would I always be remembered for just being a National champion?

As the fight went on I could feel the points going up in my head. I was landing punches. I knew I'd won when the bell rang at the end of the final round. I dropped to my knees, I had finally qualified for an Olympic Games. It's all I ever wanted and I had done it. It was an incredible moment in my life and one that I will never forget.

I've always said to myself I won my Olympic medal at the qualifiers in Athens, I just went to Beijing to collect it. The hardest part for me was to qualify. The pressure was finally off. I'd come so close in 2004 but hadn't qualified. I was in Germany at a pre-Olympics training camp with Andy Lee but when it came to the Games he headed for Athens and I headed home. I was older and more experienced and sick that I hadn't qualified. Four years later, it was a very different story as I stepped into the ring in Beijing. That medal of course is up there with my greatest days and is very special to me. I remember sitting in Dundrum shopping centre a few years later and enjoying a coffee with Pete Taylor. As I looked over, who was coming up the escalator but the great Jimmy Magee. We gave him a shout and he came over and joined us. 'How many people in this shopping centre have been to an Olympic Games as a spectator?' Jimmy asked.

'How many have represented Ireland as an Olympian in this shopping centre?' Then he said 'how many have a medal here?'

He was basically making the point that what I had achieved was indeed a rarity and something incredibly special. I know that now. Boxing was a team effort. We trained together, we eat together, and we slept together even though we never got in the ring together. After that Olympic final, we went down to the Irish bar and had drinks with family and friends.

The atmosphere was crazy when we got home with all the celebrations. It was just mental. So, when London came around I brought my mother in to speak to the team and their parents about what happens at an Olympic Games and what happens after if you are successful.

I had a power point about dealing with the media, etc. My dad was with me in Beijing in 2008 but my mother stayed at home because she didn't like flying. As I was doing well the media interest grew and grew. My house at home became a TV centre for the Irish and International media. My mother was making tea and sandwiches for all. It was just crazy. It got to a stage where members of the media would leave their tripod in the middle of the sitting room, tape it to the floor and leave. Mad stuff. At one stage, my mother ended up watching Coronation Street through a tripod. Crazy stuff. She was on her own and didn't know any better. My dad went home early and sadly missed the final. Mam was been bombarded and needed the help. It's just so important that the parents of the athletes are aware of such scenarios. We did the same again ahead of the 2016 Rio Olympics.

Most people will be surprised to hear that my toughest day was the 2008 Olympic final because it was the end of my dream. Even if I'd won gold that day I still would have felt the same because my dream of competing at an Olympic Games was over.

I don't think any athlete should feel like that when you get to a final and win a medal but that's how I felt. Getting beaten by Joe Ward for the first time in 2011 at the National Finals was a low point too. He was only 17. I was disgusted and bitterly disappointed as it was my first time getting beaten in the Seniors. He beat me convincingly the following year and again in 2013.

I miss the craic and I miss the banter that goes with boxing. I don't miss living out of a suitcase. I don't miss the travelling that's involved in being a full-time athlete.

I was incredibly lucky to have the best mother in the world because I was actually living at home during my best years as a boxer. To be able to come home after being away boxing was everything to me.

I didn't have to worry about cooking, washing or paying a mortgage. I was so lucky and I'll certainly never forget that. I miss competing and I miss seeing the joy on people's faces but that was then and this is now. I'm in a good place and very happy in my own shoes. I can sleep at night soundly.

TOMÁS Ó SÉ

Tomás Ó Sé retired from inter-county football in 2013. He won five All Ireland Senior football medals.

He also won an incredible 10 Munster Senior football championship medals and is a five time All Star award winner.

He's regarded as one of the best wing backs ever to play the game, winning the "Footballer of the Year" award in 2004.

Since he retired he's enjoyed a very successful career in the media and is a regular pundit on RTÉ's 'The Sunday Game'.

Tomás lives in Cork with Orla and children.

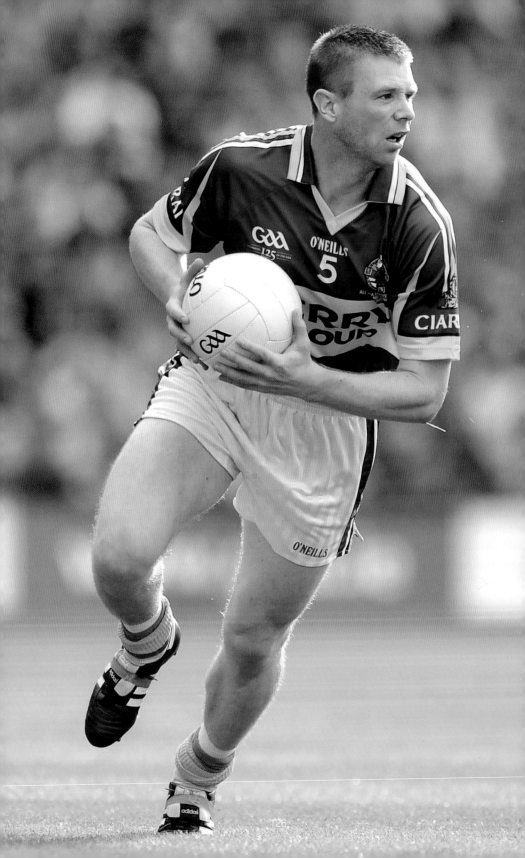

"Tomás had the unique combination of possessing a warrior mentality while also being a footballer of rare ability."

EAMONN FITZMAURICE

TOMÁS Ó SÉ

I retired in 2013 after losing to Dublin in the All Ireland Senior Football Semi-Final. That defeat still hurts.

I don't lie awake at night thinking about it but I still feel I could have done another year. Four years on, I still ask myself the question could I, should I and if I had, would I have performed at the same level? Probably not. I've always been an incredibly competitive person so wouldn't have enjoyed a lesser role.

A lot of footballers mull over retirement and take their time. Deep down, I think they know but just prolong it. For me, it wasn't a difficult decision. Shortly after the final whistle in 2013, I knew that was it for me. It was in my head that Summer but I certainly wasn't thinking about it in the build up to an All-Ireland Football Semi-Final against the Dubs. I was hoping to be in an All-Ireland Final that September but it didn't happen. I think every footballer wants to go out on a high, which is natural in sport. Before I retired I spoke to Kerry manager Eamonn Fitzmaurice about it and a few weeks later announced my retirement from inter-county football. I also spoke to my brother Darragh about it and, funny enough, neither of them talked me out of it. But I wasn't expecting them to either. They just said you've had a brilliant career and it's probably the right thing to do. All my life I've been my own man so I was always going to make up my own mind when it came to retirement.

I'd worn the green and gold of Kerry for 18 years playing minor football with the county in 1995. But what would I do now? How would I fill that void? I was now watching players that I'd played with from a distance and I found that hard. Should I not still be out there?

At times but not in a bad way I hoped Kerry wouldn't do as well so I wouldn't miss it as much. But I did miss it. Of course, on a serious note I hope Kerry go on and win more trophies but as long as the manager and a number of players [Kieran Donaghy, Darren O'Sullivan, etc] are involved I'll always feel connected to the team. And that can be hard.

After I retired in 2013, I found myself on a bit of a roller coaster in 2014. I joined 'The Sunday Game' and started writing a column for the Irish Independent. I really enjoyed working in the media. It was a different kind of buzz for me so it helped greatly in filling the void. I didn't miss football too much and certainly didn't miss the league. However, when it came to the summer and the championship I really missed it. As a player, I always loved reading the papers and listening to the pundits in the build up to big games. I loved the fact they were talking about us. I was in the Kerry bubble. But now retired, I was looking at it from a totally different perspective. I was outside looking in and a pundit myself. As Kerry progressed to the semi-final and then final in 2014 I found it very hard. I missed the buzz of putting on that Kerry jersey and playing. I remember getting into the elevator the night Kerry won the 2014 All Ireland and meeting a supporter. "You stupid fool" he said, "you should have stayed on for another year and you would have won another medal." Perhaps he was right but I'd made my own bed.

Despite working in the media, I really do miss playing football. I miss the buzz, the excitement and the big games. For me nothing will ever replace that.

I retired from every grade in 2013, including club football. It was a massive change from playing with Kerry and being part of something special. However, after 12 months out I was itching to play again and joined Nemo Rangers in Cork just twenty minutes from Fota Island where I live with Orla and family. Despite being in my late thirties, I was still competitive, I was still performing and I still wanted to be first in the runs. It sounds ridiculous I know but that's me.

I marked a player in a club game in 2016, who was twenty-one years younger than me and I survived. I was still in good shape and enjoying football again. I don't think that competitiveness will ever leave me. It's funny but I'm not competitive when it comes to other things in life such as playing golf, etc. But whatever it is about the big round ball it certainly brings out the competitor in me.

I love the GAA and will always be involved in some form be it in the media or in management. Of course, I still love playing but maybe it's time I got some sense and walked away for good. I still love going to games and enjoyed watching Marc in 2016 in his final year. 2017 was the first year none of us were involved so it was an end of an era. We've had some journey with Kerry. I love what the county stands for, I love the great players we've produced throughout the years and I love the tradition.

My greatest day in a Kerry jersey was my first All-Ireland Senior football medal in 2000 beating Galway after a replay [apologies to the author]. Croke Park was under construction at the time and so the cup was presented on the pitch. Afterwards we got to do a lap of honour which was incredibly special. We also got to meet or family and friends as we circled the stadium. Those are moments I'll never forget.

2009 was also a brilliant year as we beat our neighbours and old rivals Cork in the final. Yes, we had beaten them 2 years earlier in the decider, but this was different. It was a tough year. We had battled our way through the qualifiers and came incredibly close to exiting the championship in Sligo but for Diarmuid Murphy's heroic penalty save in the second half. The whole country thought we were finished. Myself and Colm 'Gooch' Cooper hit the headlines for all the wrong reasons but I still felt we could win another All Ireland. I was also playing some of the best football of my life. I won footballer of the year in 2004 but I felt I was going better five years later. When the whistle went at the end of the 2009 final it was one of the best feelings I've ever had. It was just perfect. It was a real case of fingers up to all those who doubted us and had written us off. We showed unbelievable strength and courage to get back on track and get over the line to win another All-Ireland. Our mental strength certainly got us through that year. We should have been beaten by Sligo, played badly against Antrim but then destroyed the Dubs in the semi-final. Football is a funny old game sometimes.

I was never a man to do things normally after winning matches. I always loved doing my own thing. I loved hanging out with my own friends and celebrating my way. A winning dressing-room is great.

It's funny you'd go a full week celebrating after winning an All-Ireland but for me the best part is the 20 minutes after the game. Why? Because you don't get a minute's privacy once you leave that room unless you leave the country. That first 20 minutes you're with the people you've been with all year. The people you've soldiered with through the good times and the bad. That core group of 40 or 50 who have all played their part. There's such a great sense of achievement. You can't replace that. You might have played a full seventy minutes but you're on such a high you could easily go out and play another.

A losing dressing room is very simply the opposite. You just want to get out of there. You just want to evaporate. Sport isn't everything but when you train that hard and get beaten it is everything. You'll always find at least three hundred reasons as to why you lost. And then the post mortem starts. I just wanted to go back to training, get back on the field and get it out of my system be it club or county. But it can be hard with no guarantees of making it the following year. Nobody remembers who lost a final. They just remember the winners. That's sport. I lost five All Ireland finals so I lost just as much as I won. I know it's a cliché but you certainly learn a lot more from losing then from winning. However, I never look back at the video afterwards.

My hardest year was 2002, when we lost to Armagh in the All Ireland Final. It was a very tough year personally as my father passed away. Football gave me an outlet to escape that year and it certainly helped. Darragh was captain, my uncle Páidí Ó Sé was the manager and it was just great. We played very well for most of 2002 only to lose to Armagh in the decider. That defeat was hard to take. It had been a tough year off the pitch and all that emotion came spilling out after that game. I would have loved to see my brother Darragh lifting the Cup that year. He was the best footballer in the country in 2002 and felt he deserved it.

However, we all know you don't get what you deserve in sport. Losing to Tyrone over the years also hurt. Every time we played them I was sure we had the beating of them but they were a tough team and a great team winning three All Ireland's between 2003 and 2008. That defeat in 2008 was heart breaking and one that really sickened me.

I don't think I've fully come to terms with retiring but maybe as the years go on it will get a little easier. I still feel so connected to something that brought me so much joy and satisfaction throughout the years. I don't think I fully appreciated everything, the big days, the success, etc when I was playing because when you're playing you have to be so focused on one thing where as when you're not playing you look at it all so differently.

I met great people, visited great places and have wonderful memories. I enjoyed every minute and for me that's the most important thing.

SONIA O'SULLIVAN

Sonia O'Sullivan is a former World champion and Olympic Silver medallist.

She's regarded as one of Ireland's greatest ever sportspeople, winning gold medals at the World and European Athletic Championships. She's also a two-time World Cross Country Champion.

She was chef de mission for the Irish Olympic Team at the 2012 Games in London.

From Cobh in County Cork, Sonia lives in Melbourne but spends some of her time in Ireland.

She's married to Nic. They have two daughters Ciara and Sophie.

"Sonia totally believed in herself. Her devotion to detail was unmatched during her career."

MARCUS O'SULLIVAN

SONIA O'SULLIVAN

I found retiring hard as I still felt I still had something to give. I think every athlete feels this way when it comes to retirement. I love athletics and have wonderful memories of doing something I loved. In the end, I retired because of injury. Looking back, maybe I trained too hard in my final years when less was enough. If I'd just kept going at a lower pace than the pace I knew, then perhaps my career would have lasted longer. I announced my retirement from athletics in February 2007 at the age of thirty-seven.

However, it was short lived. Later that year, I travelled to the 'Big Apple' and ran in the New York marathon. Two years earlier, I had competed at the London Marathon for the first time and finished 8th in a personal best of two hours, twenty-nine minutes, one second which would have been good enough to get on any team. In America I felt great, was under no pressure and had I ran around the twenty-six-mile course a minute faster that day I would have qualified automatically for the 2008 Olympic Games in Beijing, but this was never in my thoughts, I was just out for a long run. Based on that performance, and how I felt, I decided to keep going. Retirement was off the table again. I always believed there was one more thing in me but it just didn't happen.

I don't think I ever officially retired from athletics, it just gradually happened over time. I always enjoyed training and keeping fit but after I finished competing it did take a long time to come to terms with the fact that exercise was now just part of my normal life and not actual training. I do it these days because it makes me feel good. There's no end goal now, it's just a general well-being thing. After I retired, I took part in numerous 'fun runs' around the country. The first couple of times I was beaten, I questioned myself and I questioned my performance. I quickly realised that it was ok to come second or third or outside the top ten. At the end of the day, I was no longer fighting for medals. I had no times to meet for qualification and I wasn't going to re-write any record books.

It is hard for sportspeople to retire. You just never want to let go. I think it's even harder when it comes to athletics because you continue running, doing park runs, fun runs and even though these are nice events to do they can still evoke a bit of competitiveness which is fine as long as I change the parameters and expectations and find a personal goal to chase and be satisfied with. However, you certainly don't get the same buzz from it. It's funny, people still think you're there [at fun runs] to compete and to win which is not the case at all. People still see me to this day as a person who can do anything on a World level be it running, cycling or swimming.

The best thing for me about retirement was not having to train twice a day. As a professional athlete, you're also very restricted in what you can do, what you can eat, there's always the thought in the back of your mind that you need to be looking after yourself and weighing up daily decisions. Now retired there were no more regimented training mornings, no more early nights and no more restrictions. I now had choices. I could run when I wanted to run. I could eat what I wanted to eat. When you're an athlete there are people you run with, train with, your life revolves around training camps and races, following the sun and racing seasons. It's hard to make connections and set down roots anywhere as you are always on the move. However, when you retire you must find a new social group and this often evolves from meeting other parents at school and children sporting events. It can take a while to establish a new lifestyle but continuing to stay fit and joining different sports groups helps a lot with this. I have my swimming friends, cycling friends and running friends, life becomes busy again you fill your time but never the same end line that you get when chasing Olympic dreams and fast times. You don't have the same check points of reassurance along the way.

I never really missed being a professional athlete after I retired. For me it was more about finding a purpose in my life after it. I didn't miss travelling or competing but looking back at it now maybe I should have appreciated a bit more. It was an incredible journey. It certainly wasn't as intense as it is now. Today everything is a lot more measured and a lot more serious.

For me it never felt like a job. I was doing something I loved and it was a bonus that I got paid for it. I didn't have any plan or structure in place after I retired even though I do think it's important. Ironically it was the same thing with running. Growing up I didn't have a plan either, I didn't think about representing Ireland or competing at the Olympics. It was always a stepping stone for me, moving onto the next level and not looking too far ahead. Athletics is a tough sport full of ups and downs and it certainly tested me at times.

It's 2017 and I still haven't totally found a new structure in my life. I still exercise most days which is important to me so that's probably the structure. I do one hours exercise every day and I'm happy with that. However, it's easier to do other things around that now and enjoy myself a lot more. The pressure is certainly off. Nowadays I have two different lives. I have my life in Ireland and my life in Australia. Life 'Down Under' centres around my two girls and going to school, normal household jobs, cooking, cleaning and shopping. When I was a professional athlete I couldn't do a lot of stuff with them as I was busy training and often away. Sometimes I do feel a bit guilty about that but since retirement we've spent a lot more time together and get on great. They're my life now. I also enjoy doing analysis on television from time to time and writing for The Irish Times. I also have different groups that I coach and advise, school kids, club runners and a few new to running. I feel I have a greater understanding of training now than when I was competing at the highest level and I try to spread this understanding around as it's not all about out the door as fast as you can!

Looking back, it's fair to say I had two careers, before 1996 and after 1996 where I approached things very differently and appreciated things a lot more. My greatest day was not a championship win or my silver medal at the 2000 Olympic Games. They're the obvious ones. I achieved what I set out to achieve in those competitions. 1994 was a very special year in my life. In Edinburgh that year I broke the 2000m world record in a time of five minutes, twenty-five seconds. That record stood until it was broken indoors in 2017, still no one has run so fast outdoors.

A week later in London I broke the European 3000m in a time of eight minutes, twenty-one seconds. I just felt unstoppable at the time, it was all about racing and I living the dream. I just had the ability to go to another level when it was needed in a race. I felt I had this extra boost in the closing stages to pull away and win comfortably. I never worried about the last 400 metres because I knew if I was there I was in with a great chance of winning. I could do no wrong. I look back now and wonder just how did I do that.

1998 was also a great year for me as I won both the short and long course events at the World Cross Country Championships in Marrakech followed by double gold at the European Championships in Budapest. After a couple of difficult years including the 1996 Olympic Games in Atlanta I was back on top of the world after being written off by many. I felt great.

After winning a medal I would always run back to the hotel. Literally run back. Anytime we were competing abroad one of the first things I'd do is find out how far it was from the hotel to the stadium. I would then recruit people to run back with me. This was nearly more important than the actual race. I would use it as a warm down. Once back at the hotel I would go for an ice bath followed by dinner and the occasional glass of red wine with my team. And that was it. You were back training the following day.

There were tough days too.

The earlier part of 1996 wasn't too bad but the Olympic Games was a disaster. However, when I look back now at what happened in Atlanta it wasn't a defining moment for me. The following year I was just trying to make up for it all and picked up a couple of medals. I was enjoying training again, I had a new coach but unfortunately my mind wasn't in tune with my body. I was very frustrated. I didn't qualify for the 5000m final in Athens in 1997 but it didn't overly concern me. For the first time ever I was happy not to make the final because I didn't really want to go out and run again. I didn't feel right, I wasn't ready and my head wasn't in it. I was also in the final of the 1500m that week but again things didn't go well. I finished 8th. Shortly after that race I rang Alan Storey, my coach in London. He just said, "you've got to stop now, take a break you've had enough for this year." I was at a point where I wasn't enjoying it and stopping certainly sounded attractive. I bounced back in 1998 re-energised and re-focussed.

When I look back on my career I often wonder could I have done things differently or anyway better. But I guess all sportspeople do the same. I'm happy, I've had a great life to date and have wonderful memories. It's hard for me to get away from athletics as I'm married to Nic [Bideau] who coaches and manages athletes in Australia. One of our girls Sophie enjoys athletics at school and with her local running group. I see certain things of me in her. She always runs well if a race is important to her. She's fifteen and competes in the eight hundred and fifteen hundred metres and cross country in the winter. At the moment it's very much a social thing for her. I just let her work away and never put any pressure on her. Sometimes I'll make comments on her races, but she'll always disagree with me, nothing better than knowing your own mind. I'm really enjoying life after sport.

EOIN REDDAN

Eoin Reddan is a former Irish rugby player who played at scrum-half. He was capped 71 times for Ireland.

Born in Limerick, Reddan played for Connacht, Munster and Leinster. He also played for Wasps in England. He made 11 appearances across three Rugby World Cup tournaments in 2007, 2011 and 2015.

He won numerous trophies including two RBS 6 Nations titles and 3 Heineken Cup crowns. He has also captained Wasps, Leinster and his country.

He lives in Dublin with wife Aoife and children Tom and Evie.

"Living proof that it's not the size of the dog in the fight but the size of the fight in the dog. Eoin excelled amongst big men with his skill, guile and chirpy resilience, combined with his desperation to win every contest."

JOE SCHMIDT

EOIN REDDAN

Life is all about choices.

In May 2016, I had to make a choice. A pretty big one. Keep playing rugby or retire and start again. I decided to retire.

I made up my mind about retiring from the sport I love during the week leading up to the Pro 12 final defeat to Connacht in Edinburgh in 2016. All season I had been afraid of deciding to retire when I wasn't playing well or the club was having a rough week. There are always tough times in sport and making big decisions at those times is never a good idea, but after the semi-final there should have been no doubt in my mind, after all I had played well and we were playing in a final but I still couldn't shake the feeling that it was time to go.

After the final, I told my Dad at the airport and he didn't believe me. But I was retiring. I met with Joe Schmidt and Leo Cullen the following Monday and told them my decision. Thankfully Joe felt he still needed me for the tour of South Africa. I was delighted and travelled to play the Springboks that Summer. In relation to Leinster I wasn't sure where I stood at the start of the year. They could easily have said goodbye and good luck to me at the end of 2016. Leo is a good friend of mine and I've always had huge respect for him. In the end, I said goodbye to Leinster and walked away in June 2016, which I know wasn't ideal for him, it being at such a late stage in the year. But as always, he was very understanding and he wished me well.

In many ways going on tour to South Africa was a great way to finish up. I really enjoyed every minute of it, winning my 71st cap in the final test. It was great having my father and brother in South Africa for that game. Dad was with me for the three weeks of the tour and my brother flew in from New York. It was magic. Meeting them at the end of the game was highly emotional, as was ringing my wife Aoife at home. They've always been there for me during the good times and the bad.

I was gutted we'd lost the game but for the first time in my life there wasn't a next week to worry about. Post-match analysis and Monday morning post mortems were now a thing of the past.

After the game, the Irish management organised a 'goodbye party' for me in the hotel, which was a lovely touch. My ten-year career with Ireland was over but I was ok. I was quite content as I knew the next chapter was also a hugely exciting one. I was moving into the world of aircraft leasing and looking forward to it. However, before all that I was going travelling with my family for ten weeks and couldn't wait.

Retirement from sport is different in many ways for every athlete. For example, in amateur sport you mightn't always get picked but you're still part of the squad and that can be the case for as long as you choose to keep playing. Professional sport is business. You either get a contract or you don't. As I got older I always wanted to be in a position where I could decide each year whether I would play on or not. I certainly didn't want to be forced into a situation where I had to play on because I couldn't do anything else or I needed the money. Or worse, not be good enough and told to leave.

As I moved into my thirties, I also began to think about life after sport a lot more. I had been tipped off by a number of people to have a look at Avolon. They are an aircraft leasing company based in Dublin. I was still playing rugby at the time and it was a long shot but I felt Avolon could be a very interesting place to work post rugby.

Today I work full time with the company as a business analyst with the responsibility for the pricing and structuring of aircraft acquisitions, aircraft sales, placement of aircraft and capital raising. I was used to things happening quickly and continuously, the next training session, the next match, squad selection and my role in Avolon is no different.

There are so many similar traits in both the sporting world and business. Ambition, competition, it's fast moving, etc. I was used to competing to win trophies and now I am part of a new team trying to succeed in a new field and I love it.

So, in May 2016 it was a case of playing on or taking that job in Avolon. I slept on it for a few nights but deep down I knew this opportunity was too good to pass up. When I joined the company and started the new job I knew I'd made the right decision. I'd thought long and hard about both options and both looked good to be honest.

But I had to make a decision.

One was ultimately the end of something and one was the start of something else. I did have a couple of sleepless nights thinking about retiring and life after sport but once I started to go to bed thinking about my new life, the new challenges, new goals outside of rugby then I knew was time to go.

I don't miss the matches. Some players do but I don't. I'd love to say I enjoyed every minute of my career but I didn't. No matter who we played I always felt huge pressure to win and to play well. Each match presented something different. Will this game help me get on the Irish team, will we win another trophy, it is a step to something bigger, etc? I always felt that anytime I relaxed and tried to enjoy rugby I was way off the game physically. I'm only about 80kgs so it would take me days to get ready for a game and get ready for a fight. I don't miss that.

I miss training and all that goes with it in preparing for battle. When you're a rugby player you've one single focus in your life and that's rugby whereas in work you might have ten or fifteen different things to do in a day.

You'd be complaining about having to do the shopping or go the post office which is funny. As a rugby player, you can happily lie down for three or four hours during the day because it's for something, it's part of your preparation ahead of a big match at the weekend. You don't feel like you're wasting time.

Every decision you make is based around the game. Nothing else comes into it and to let anything else into it would be unprofessional so you don't. I don't miss all that. I can now do other things in my life that I know it won't affect my game. This year Aoife and I went to Paris for a weekend and I was able to walk around the city. I didn't have to conserve my energy for training on Monday morning and take taxi's everywhere.

I make a big effort to stay in touch with a lot of the players. In my view when you leave it's up to you to maintain those relationships. It's not up to them to feel sorry for you and be ringing you to see how you're doing with life after rugby. I know what they're doing and I know how consuming it is to be in that bubble.

I know the challenges they face every week. I know when a player doesn't get picked on a Tuesday for a match for what might be perceived as a run of the mill game the following Saturday that most people think the player doesn't mind but it's the opposite. He's eating up inside and desperately disappointed. So, the last thing he's thinking about it ringing a former player or team mate.

I love watching Ireland and Leinster. I'm at ease with my retirement and enjoying a new life now. I watched Ireland beat New Zealand in Chicago in 2016 and was over the moon for the lads.

Shortly after I retired, I went along to a few games with my dad to see what it was like. I got the special treatment from Leinster, got great tickets and ended up sitting in beside the subs. I just felt a bit uncomfortable about the whole thing as I was no longer involved with the club. So, the next time I went I told nobody, got two tickets myself and sat in the uncovered stand with my son Tom. Nobody knew I was going, no one noticed me and to me that's what's called moving on. I was okay with all that. I was still a friend and supporter to the lads I was watching, but I was no longer a player. I think it's important to actively seek out losing that image you have in your head of being a player and to understand what the reality is and how that should work.

I started off my career playing rugby with Connacht while also studying in Limerick so I got into a habit of doing both. I always wanted to do both because at the time rugby wasn't paying much so I wasn't going to be earning a lot. I also thought at that stage I would need a job after rugby anyway. I graduated in UL with a degree in Business studies, accountancy and finance and ended up signing for Munster for two years.

I took a break from any further studies and quickly became obsessed with the game. I was thinking about rugby twenty-four seven, thinking about training, thinking about getting picked, thinking about not getting picked but much to my disappointment my contract was not renewed. I was devastated.

I know now I'd got the balance wrong. Most people work in an office all week and go to the gym three times a week. I worked in the gym all week but really, I needed to be doing something like a part time job or another course to balance things up. I moved to Wasps and started studying again before moving back to Ireland to join Leinster. When I returned home, I was keen to keep up my studies. I was always thinking about improving my CV as well as getting the balance right. Indeed, while studying I met with people from Avolon in 2013 and realised from that meeting that I was way off where I needed to be. My mother Geraldine who sadly passed away in 2010, my father Don and my wife Aoife have always been hugely supportive throughout the years as have my four brothers Donal, Diarmuid, Alan and Cian.

I wouldn't describe my career as smooth. To have people behind you like my family who really believe in you is a very important factor.

In 2013, when all eyes were on the Aviva for Ireland's showdown with New Zealand I was sitting on the bench in Italy against Treviso. I was due to be on the bench for the All Blacks game but was dropped that week. It was Joe's first Autumn series and he obviously had his own reasons for doing it. I was gutted. To be fair to him, he offered me the chance to stay on site with the lads at the hotel.

I spoke to Aoife about it and she was pretty adamant that I shouldn't be waiting around for anyone and I should definitely go and play in Italy.

After much consideration, I agreed and decided to travel. I rang my dad to tell him the bad news and to enjoy the game at the Aviva.

Five hours later he rang me to say he'd cancelled his tickets and was going to Italy. He travelled on our flight. It meant so much that he had decided that watching me sit on the bench in Treviso was more important than seeing Ireland attempt to beat NZ for the first time ever in the Aviva. I played well against Treviso and certainly it made a difference that he had made such a huge effort to come and see me play. Rugby is full of key moments but that match turned out to be a huge turning point in my season.

I've enjoyed some great moments throughout my rugby career. Winning my first trophy with Wasps Rugby Club was special. We won the Anglo-Welsh Cup at Twickenham in 2006 beating Llanelli Scarlets and for the first time in my life I realised that there was nothing wrong with me. Up to that moment I had never won a single trophy at any level of rugby and I was twenty-five. Was there something wrong with me? All those questions I'd asked myself as a rugby player had been answered. To most, it wasn't the biggest game in the world but to me it was massive. I had finally won a rugby medal and it was very special.

I went onto win the Heineken Cup with Wasps in 2007 beating Leicester in the final and scoring a try on the day. My whole family were there to witness it including my mother who was sick at the time. She travelled on the team bus with me afterwards, which was very special and incredibly emotional.

To win an ERC medal was great. It was the currency in Ireland at the time following the success of both Ulster and Munster in the competition. If you didn't have one you hadn't reached the required standard.

There was always huge pressure on players joining a club like Wasps and winning trophies. The club's mentality was very simple. You've joined a great club but what have you put in the cabinet. It didn't matter what the club had won in the past. It was a real case of what have we won since you got here.

Internationally there were some magical days too. Beating England in the Aviva in 2011 when they were trying to win a grand slam was incredible. Beating Australia in the 2011 Rugby World Cup in New Zealand was also a high point. I played for fifty-five minutes of that game before being substituted. I didn't play again for the remainder of the competition which was hugely disappointing and incredibly frustrating.

As a professional athlete, there are plenty of ups and downs. That was one of the lowest points in my career. I had been playing well in the build up to the World Cup and things were going well. I started against Australia but being taken off really hurt. Up to that point I could see ways of improving so that I could become a regular in the team. However, despite playing well in such a big game Declan Kidney was now going another way - I felt at that point that he was never going to see me as Ireland's first choice scrum half. I felt I had proved myself to him and couldn't do anymore. I get on well with Declan now but he obviously had his reasons for not picking me. Coaches can try and summarise and give you a couple of reasons as to why you're not playing. But I find it's often hard for them to explain their decision properly to you.

When you break these disappointments down you always have to put the team first. You want the team to win because the longer the team is in the competition the more the chance you have to get back on and the longer the team is in the competition the more the chance of winning a big trophy.

As a rugby player, it's so important to enjoy the good days. However most of the time it was just pure relief. All the pressure and expectation was gone. I don't think I ever won anything where I was surprised we'd won. I learnt as much from winning as I did from losing. It was a real case of knowing how to win. To do all the right preparation and lose is mind blowing and dangerous for athletes. Just what do you do now if that isn't working? I was never looking for the perfect formula to winning because in sport it doesn't exist. You have a role, you go out and do it to the best of your ability and you hope you get over the line. Having the patience and confidence to stick to a plan and trust your team mates is central to winning big matches and there is no better way of learning this than by winning while employing this philosophy. Teams that win doing this will often enter a longer period of success than those who won due to players one off moments of brilliance. Teams who have both are usually on a different level.

If you're thinking about retiring, finding what you want to do is the hard bit. Go work in a coffee shop or an office, etc for a week and give yourself a chance of finding the thing you like. Because if you find the thing you like then it plays a huge part in filling that void. Some people might like to do one thing, others a number of things.

During my career I tried different jobs for a few weeks. At the end, I knew they weren't for me, and this was very helpful when it came to actually picking something. Some players take up roles in clubs, others go to college, some do media. There are plenty of options for retired athletes.

My advice would be to get busy finding out what you'd like to do, try things and don't be afraid. It's normal not knowing immediately what you want to do. It's not something to be worrying about. Get out there, meet people, use your contacts, start conversations. Find the thing that will give you the best chance of being happy when you retire from sport.

DONAL ÓG CUSACK

Donal Óg Cusack is a former Cork hurler. He won 3 All Ireland Senior Hurling titles and 2 All Star Awards.

He's regarded as one of the greatest goalkeepers ever to play the game.

Born in Cloyne, he won All Ireland medals at Minor, Under 21, Intermediate and Senior Level.

He also made 54 championship appearances, which is a record for a Cork goalkeeper.

He's been chairman of the Gaelic Players Association and has worked as a pundit with RTÉ's The Sunday Game.

Donal became a coach with the Clare Senior hurling team in 2015. He lives in Cork.

"Donal Og is one of the most courageous people I know and he demonstrated this on the field and off the field on many an occasion."

DONAL O'GRADY

DONAL ÓG CUSACK

Retirement is a like being in a warzone and all of a sudden a man taps you on the shoulder and goes 'Did you not know today was your day to go?' Surprised, you reply "I thought I had another couple of months left here." The next minute you're whipped away in a helicopter from the madness and the following day you're reading about it in the newspaper. It's not your war anymore, despite being in the thick of it twenty-four hours earlier.

I never actually retired.

Jimmy Barry-Murphy, former Cork Senior Hurling Manager dropped me in February 2013. I had a sense it was coming. Ten months earlier, I got badly injured rupturing my achilles tendon against Tipperary in Thurles. I was captain and things had been going well. Jimmy visited me at home in Cloyne and just said "get yourself back, you know the drill. You're a big boy." "There are no guarantees" he said but "you'll get your shot again." I spent most of 2012 recovering and returned to Cork training ahead of the 2013 season. It was good to be back but I was getting a sense that I wasn't in his plans going forward. As I drove back from Dublin days later the phone rang and it was Jimmy. He asked to meet me and we did so in a car park on the road to Ringaskiddy. "I'm letting you go" he said but I pleaded with him not to and was happy to stay with the panel even as third choice goalkeeper. I wanted to fight my way back to being number 1 again. He said "no I've made my decision." We shook hands and off he went. I was in fierce condition and had bounced back from a terrible injury and certainly didn't want my county career ending there.

I'd worked incredibly hard all year to get back for the 2013 season. I'd spent endless hours and days in Paírc Uí Chaoimh running up those steps just to get right. I would train at lunchtime and around my busy work schedule. It was hard, really hard at times but I loved playing for Cork.

But the meeting with Jimmy meant I wasn't going back and it hurt. It was a horrible way to go. To make it worse, I was actually back and in the Cork dressing room at the start of the year and had trained with the team. But I knew the way Jimmy was looking back at me.

I just knew that look.

The following day I was on a plane to the USA with the GPA, so had very little time to think about the disappointing news. I was sitting in reception at Fitzpatrick's Hotel in New York when I looked up and noticed the RTÉ News Now channel on the television. There was a ticker at the bottom of the screen with the words 'Donal Óg Cusack dropped from Cork panel.' It certainly was a surreal moment. None of my group knew about it except Pat Gilroy, the former Dublin football manager who I'd told earlier in the day. It was just mad. Here I was thousands of miles away from home and I couldn't get away from it.

2013 was a very different year. I wasn't training and playing with the Cork Senior hurlers for the first time in 17 years. But I was busy with work and joined The Sunday Game in RTÉ which helped hugely in dealing with the void. I loved being involved and took a huge interest in the analysis side of things. I was finished with Cork, I was no longer involved, it was not my fight anymore and this was a new challenge. I found it remarkable the amount of attention the show got, what we said, what we wore... I really enjoyed my time with RTÉ until I joined Davy Fitzgerald and the Clare backroom team in 2015.

Growing up, I always dreamed about playing hurling and wearing the red of Cork. I always dreamed about competing at the top level and playing in All Ireland Finals. It's all I ever wanted to do.

I was always happiest thinking about hurling and visualising the games, the moments and the big days. I'd be thinking about it in the car with my father. As I got older, I'd think about it while spending time with friends. I'd even think about it in the shower. But when I was let go by Cork in 2013 it all disappeared. The dreaming was over. It was like a switch.

I was no longer playing with Cork so there was nothing to dream about anymore. It took a long time to come to terms with being let go and no longer involved. It's just so hard when you've spent most of your life dreaming about something and being so passionate about something such as hurling and suddenly it's over.

Nothing ever matches playing, competing and captaining your own county. In some way, I try and match it at work as I lead a team of people who report to me from the USA and from many parts of Europe. It's a very competitive environment so it is a bit like playing but it's still not the same and never will be. There's just a rawness and a recklessness and a lawlessness and a beauty about sport. It's almost like a war.

I remember the build up to games, the day itself and just being on a different planet. Nothing else matters for those seventy minutes. As a player, I did think about life after sport a couple of times during my career. I remember saying to former Cork hurling manager John Allen at one stage "We'll look back at these days and these moments in years to come as the best days of our life." We'd a great team at the time, we'd great leaders too and took responsibility for our actions and indeed our performances. We also knew that these great days weren't going to last forever.

Someday it would be all over.

As All Ireland winning captain, Seán Óg Ó'hAilpin said one day "What you love too much will end up killing us and this game will kill us we love it so much." It was so true.

Not being involved in Cork would also have an impact on my father. He had bred me as a hurler and was always hugely supportive. In some respects, it's nearly harder for family members when you're playing as they worry about you, constantly think about you and are always there for you. They've been on a journey too and suddenly that journey is over.

Despite not lining out for Cork, I was still playing with my club but I found it very hard going back after finishing with the county.

I struggled a lot with it. I lost interest in training, I had lost my motivation and I found it hard to connect with the squad. It was no longer the biggest thing or most important thing in my life. I was no longer dreaming.

Despite my struggles with retirement, I was mentally prepared for it. I had read a lot about it, the process, what they go through, coming to terms with it. It was part of my job at the GPA. To me, it seems like a lot of people leave their sport with a bitter taste. They feel they could have given more and perhaps achieved more. That's why it's so important that there is a players' movement to help and understand life after sport.

Education is key. Every player who retires gets a letter from the GPA saying, 'congratulations on your career' and here are our contact details. It's so important that players have a dual career when playing so they're in a good position work wise come retirement. It can be very difficult with such a demanding schedule. A lot of players find themselves starting jobs alongside others in a company and when they retire from playing they are two to three steps behind them due to their massive commitment and time spent training and playing with the county.

It's essential you look after the other side of the house as well while playing. It's also important to identify the strengths that made you a good sportsperson and take them into your professional career at work. It's amazing how a lot of great sportspeople don't recognise what qualities made them good.

I have so many great memories, from playing with Cork but one that stands out for me is shortly after the 2005 All Ireland Senior Hurling Final victory over Galway and sitting on the team bus beside Brian Corcoran. We had just won back to back All Ireland's and we were both over the moon.

That sense of total satisfaction. A few days later, we were sitting inside a pub in Cork watching the match at 3am in the morning. It was such a great feeling looking back at it like we'd never seen it. We had a great set up then, we were a team of fanatics and we were already looking forward to 2006 and the possibility of a three in a row.

Twelve months later. we were sitting in the bus in tears. We had just lost the final to Kilkenny and it hurt. Every time you're beaten, it's a bad day. They are two very different dressing rooms. People think you're exaggerating but it's like a death in the family when you lose. It's the same process you go through, the same grieving, the same feeling. I hated losing.

I miss the purpose of it all. Everybody in life is after a sense of purpose. It's such a healthy pursuit and in doing so you're also bringing a huge amount of honour to your family in that pursuit.

When I look back on my career now I am hugely grateful for everything I achieved and the great people I met along the way. I loved the process. I loved going training. I loved the competitiveness of training. I loved the fulfilment it gave me in life. I loved playing for Cork. I still miss it.

I haven't retired, I was just dropped.

A.P. MCCOY

A.P. McCoy is a former Irish jockey and one of the greatest of all time. He retired in 2015.

He was Champion jockey a record 20 consecutive times riding an incredible 4,357 winners throughout his career.

McCoy rode his first winner in 1992 at 17 years of age before going on to win the Cheltenham Gold Cup, the Champion Hurdle and the English Grand National.

He now works for ITV Sport as a racing pundit.

He lives in England and is married to Chanelle. They have two children Eve and Archie.

"A. P. McCoy was a ferocious competitor on the race track but an extraordinary human being in other circumstances.**"**

JIM BOLGER

A.P. MCCOY

Life after racing is ok.

I was one of the lucky ones because I planned my retirement and knew if everything went to plan I was going to be retiring in April 2015. And that's what happened. I retired and am now a former jockey.

At thirty-five, I'd been Champion Jockey fifteen times and knew if I could win five more I'd still only be forty and not forty-one. I always felt jump jockeys shouldn't be riding into their forties so retiring in 2015 was the right time for me. At the start of the season, I said to J.P. McManus that it was probably going to be my last year riding professionally. I ended the 2015 season, winning my 20th Champion Jockey title. I had thought about retiring for five years so it certainly wasn't a spur of the moment decision.

But it was still a very hard decision in the end.

Most experts would say that when a jump jockey thinks about retiring they should retire. Some jump jockeys retire because they lose their nerve a little and an element of fear creeps into their racing. I never felt that way but I still knew the dangers and the fears from day one. I was a realist.

In February 2015, I announced my retirement date to the world two and a half months before my final race at Sandown. In many ways, talking about it and chatting to others helped me prepare for retirement. I knew once I announced it there was no turning back. The toughest part of it was saying those words "I'm retiring." I'm not sure you can prepare for retirement but I did the best I could in the weeks and months leading up to my final race.

My final day as a jockey is very hard to describe. The morning of April 25th, 2015 was no different to any other. I got up, did twenty minutes on the treadmill and then hopped into a hot bath for an hour. Suddenly it hit me that this indeed would be the last time I was ever going to do this.

I can stand on the scales tomorrow and it won't matter what weight I am for the first time in twenty years.

Life will just be so different in so many ways.

Over the years, I've had numerous drivers but in recent years Arnie has been with me. Every morning for the last seven years he's been pulling up outside my front door to bring me racing. He wouldn't be picking me up tomorrow. He's also become a very good friend. In my final race, I finished third on a horse called Box Office. And that was it. My life as a jockey was over. I was tired, when I returned home that night as I had invited a lot of people back to our local hotel for a party. I also had another party at the house the following day for friends, etc. It was so surreal. I was now retired. I was now a former jockey.. I went to Punchestown to meet friends and people were still talking about my retirement, but it was fine. I could now eat what I wanted to eat and not worry about the next day and making the correct weight. But after a week or ten days all that suddenly began to wear off.

I've heard that 'a sportsperson is the only person that dies twice.' This is so true. For twenty years, I got up every morning with the fear that I might not be any good, with a goal, with a challenge and with an expectation of myself from myself. There was also huge expectation to perform for the people who employed me to ride their horses. I always wanted to perform for myself but I always wanted to perform for them as well.

When I get up in the morning now and I don't have that expectation I just think what's the point, what has my life come to, how do I replace racing, with what and how do I get that intensity back? But the reality of it is that it's not coming back. I often have days when I think there must be something that can replace being a jockey but realistically I don't think there's anything that I'd love to do as much as racing. I was so lucky to be doing something for so long that wasn't a job where as from now on everything I do is going to feel like a job. It's going to feel like I'm working. I've never done a day's work in my life.

Life after sport is very different now. It's like flicking a switch.

I spoke to my agent Dave Roberts three or four times a day, every day for the past 20 years. He booked all my races. Now I speak to him once a month. I no longer meet the lads who looked after my gear for over twenty years. Indeed, if I want to see them I have to call them out from the weigh-room, as I'm no longer allowed inside the four walls at the racecourse.

There are days when I find retirement difficult especially if I'm home for a day or two and just thinking too much. I find myself watching the racing on television and thinking should I still be out there, I'm still as good as a lot of them lads riding. I find myself doing the silliest of things just to keep busy. Since I retired I've been doing some media work with ITV racing. That has certainly helped as it means I'm going to the races, I'm meeting up with people I haven't seen in a while and not sitting at home going mad. Working as a pundit also concentrates the mind and makes me watch racing knowing that I have to say something interesting afterwards or something that the audience at home might not have noticed. I enjoy being a panellist but it can be difficult at times to fill the time in between races. If you're working on soccer or rugby you talk for a couple of minutes before, at half time and after. As an analyst, it's pretty short and sweet.

Whereas if you're working at Newmarket and covering a six-furlong race that lasts for a minute you've got about twenty-eight minutes or so to fill until the next race. It can be tricky. There are only so many ways to describe a race. At the end of the day, a horse race is getting from the start to the finish line before anybody else. I often feel I'm just saying things to pass the time. It can become very repetitive.

However, I only do a small number of days, which include the big days like Cheltenham, Aintree, Epsom and Ascot. I wouldn't like to be doing it every Saturday.

Apart from working with ITV I also do some work for JP McManus and I'm President of the injured jockeys fund, which takes up a lot of time. It's hugely important as it cares for a lot of people. But all the things I'm doing doesn't replace what I loved doing for over twenty years. I often feel I'm doing stuff just to pass the time.

There are lots of times I wished I hadn't won twenty champion jockey titles, because I could have kept going and nobody would really care. Shortly after I retired trainer John Joe O'Neill had two horses running in the Cheltenham Gold Cup and Barry Geraghty got injured. O'Neill asked me to ride one of them, but I just couldn't. I was now retired and wouldn't allow myself to do it.

I've had more holidays since I retired than I had in the last twenty years. I went to the US Masters in Augusta in April 2017 for the practice days on Monday, Tuesday and Wednesday. It was great watching the best golfers in the world prepare for one of sport's biggest prizes. I also got a chance to spend some time with Padraig Harrington who was great pointing out things to me that one would never spot when playing the game. He knows Augusta very well. As a jockey, I would never have gotten the chance to go to events like that.

I miss the discipline associated with being a jockey. There is a lot of shit I miss that people would laugh at or not understand. I miss the danger, I miss the adrenalin and I miss the fear. I miss not getting up in the morning and thinking I have to lose four or five pounds and I can't have breakfast. People probably think it's great now that I don't have to worry about what I eat and making weight, but it's not. I eat now because it's a novelty whereas before eating and indeed not eating was a huge part of the job.

I'm very proud of winning twenty champion jockey titles in a row. Do I think someone will be champion jump jockey twenty years in a row in the future? I'm not sure. I'm forty-three now so that record won't be matched or indeed broken until I'm well into my sixties. Every record eventually gets broken but if it happens at that stage in my life, it won't bother me. Will someone ride 289 winners in a season? I don't know. I rode 307 winners in a calendar year. Will someone break that? I don't think so, because I don't think anyone will ever have the firepower that I had with trainer Martin Pipe. Richard Johnson has over 3,000 winners but at forty he's unlikely to reach four thousand, three hundred and fifty-seven. I was so lucky that I worked with the most successful people. To ride for people like Martin Pipe and JP McManus was just amazing. To have an agent and booker like Dave Roberts was incredible. He is a freak of nature.

I think I've had a successful career but I don't know to this day whether I underachieved or overachieved. When you're riding you have to believe you're the best. For someone to achieve something you have to have a dream, you have to have a vision, you have to have a goal. You need to have a target. I always had a target. I always had a dream. That dream was always to be champion jockey. That was always my goal.

I had amazing help along the way; People who guided and shaped me. From my early days as a child with Billy Rock who really made me believe in myself to my days with Jim Bolger. Jim instilled a lot of great things in my head that will be there forever including discipline. Toby Balding taught me about people, and how you should treat them.

Martin Pipe taught me that winning was the only thing that mattered. The likes of John Joe O'Neill and JP McManus brought a lot of normality to the whole thing. They also made me appreciate it a lot more and brought a lot of enjoyment to it. I'd say up to riding my 3,000th winner I wasn't sure if I was ok or not at racing. When I rode 4,000 winners, it was probably the first time I accepted that I'm actually all right. But I still ask myself to this day could I have done better. I rode plenty of losers too.

My greatest achievement in racing will always be beating Sir Gordon Richards record. His record was there for fifty-five years. He was the most successful jockey of all time.

Richards had beaten Fred Archie's record--a genius rider from the 1800s who in the end sadly died by suicide. Richards was so dominant for such a long time as a jump jockey, and that is incredibly difficult. You just can't afford to have injuries or suspensions. In the calendar year of 2002 when I rode 307 winners, it meant there were only 58 days in the year that I didn't ride a winner. Away from the records winning the Aintree Grand National in 2010 on 'Don't Push It' certainly gave me the greatest sense of relief. I got a huge amount of fulfilment from winning that race. It meant I'd never have to answer that question 'did you ever win the Grand National?'

There are plenty of great jockeys much better than me that never won the race such as John Francome, Peter Scudamore, John Joe O'Neill, Frank Berry and Charlie Swan. A lot of shit ones did.

In racing, there are tough days too and there were a few in my career none more so than colleagues getting badly injured or passing away.

When Richard Davis was killed at Southwell in 1996, I remember going into the ambulance room to see him and the crew telling me he was bad.

He died on the way to hospital with internal bleeding. I remember it like it was yesterday. I was champion jockey that year for the first time. I remember the day John Thomas was badly injured and had been told in the weigh-room that things aren't good by one of the doctors. He'd been resuscitated twice. I remember looking over at John's peg and his suit hanging up and thinking he's not going to be wearing that suit tonight. It was devastating.

A lot of people go on about equine tragedies but it's not the same. Even talking about it makes me cry. It was just heart breaking for his family, friends, colleagues and everybody around him. There are just certain things in your life you never forget. Life as a jockey is full of ups and downs that's for sure.

The advice I would give to someone retiring is that you've got to keep moving and looking forward. As a jockey, I never looked back at races and now that I'm retired I still don't. A very successful man and in my view the coolest man on the planet [I won't say his name] wrote me a letter when I retired. In that letter, he said 'you need to do what you did all your life, keep looking forward.'

I've no regrets. I took no short cuts and didn't miss any days. I know I went racing some days and think what possessed me to do that? I rode in Cheltenham eight weeks after I had two metal plates put in my back. That was me. I worked my bollocks off. Nothing will ever replace being a jockey. Nothing. It's the same for any sportsperson. What you need to do, is accept it as best you can and as quickly as you can.

I'll never find anything that I enjoyed as much as being a jockey. As a child, it was my dream to be a jockey. That's all I ever wanted in my life. I didn't want anything else. I didn't want to play soccer, play golf or be a rock star. I feel very lucky. I lived the dream. Not everyone can say that.

DANIEL RITCHIE

Daniel Ritchie is a former International rower who represented England.

He won gold at the 2013 World Championships in Chungju. Ritchie also won a silver medal in Karapiro at the 2010 World Championships and again in Bled in 2011.

Since retiring from rowing he has worked as a motivational speaker amongst other things.

He lives in England.

This is his story about life after sport.

DANIEL RITCHIE

As an athlete, you die twice; the first time is the day you retire. When you're an athlete that's all you know. Training, eating, sleeping, competing; what little social life there is, there's very little time remaining to look forward and think about anything else. We train for years, and in most cases it consumes our existence in many ways sacrificing our lives, and finances, moving away from friends and family, cutting short education and sacrificing romantic and personal relationships to name just a few.

Yet at some point, we all face one harsh inescapable reality: Retirement. Most choose not to think about it in great detail, but once we've achieved glory or failed to reach the heights we dreamed of it all ends, irrespective of the reasons. Everything that was sacrosanct suddenly has no relevance, instead you're left with a simple question. What next?

The answer is different for everyone, some suffer from a loss of identity, other from depression and liken retirement to the loss of a loved one, and others view it as a relief.

Personally, I took a year out of 'life', I travelled, walked my dog, went on holiday, and made some furniture. Only to be left with the same question "what next?"

Boxing legend Sugar Ray Leonard famously quoted, "Nothing could satisfy me outside the ring. There is nothing in life that can compare to becoming a world champion, having your hand raised in that moment of glory, with thousands, millions of people cheering you on."

I never had that feeling. Granted when we won the World Championships there weren't millions of people cheering, my parents did not even watch it live. But the sacrifices we made to achieve that pinnacle as a team were just as real.

Standing as a World Champion watching the Union Jack ascend the flag pole and singing the national anthem, I felt empty, devoid of any real emotion except contentment and disappointment.

I should have retired then, for reasons I need not mention. I had achieved the one goal I had strived for a decade to fulfil, but I couldn't because of – "what next?"

I was scared; Sport was all I had ever known. Firstly, as a swimmer sent to Australia by British swimming as part of their off-shore training programme and latterly dropping out of University to row. Sport was quite literally my life, and my goal was absolute, I wanted nothing more, I was willing to sacrifice anything for it, and I did.

A "tunnel vision syndrome".

The trait coaches look for, identify, and exploit. Most athletes like myself are unaware they suffer from this and instead, we spend all of our time training, competing, generating and analysing results, obsessed with the "gold standard" oblivious to the cares and frustrations of those around us.

After my career in sport, I was visibly, mentally and emotionally unprepared for the balanced perspective required of a "proper job" and career opportunities. I was depressed, I missed the applied focus to a goal, the stop at nothing, whatever it takes, culture that elite sport requires.

At that realisation, I listened to an ex-team mate, "Remember you can train skill, but you can't train personality." So instead of trying to change, I searched for a career and culture that I could thrive in.

An environment where I can train and develop new skills, where entrepreneurial spirit and the desire to get back up after a hard hit is celebrated, while the constant striving for balance and caring more about the team is paramount. Most importantly, a career where I could display a sincere desire to overcome mistakes, make amends, and do better each day not only for myself but for the team.

My life is now a world away from boats, oars, tight lycra, large swathes of discomfort, and the occasional wailing from a mega phone.

It's replaced by a desk, computer, telephone, database and network of contacts. I now work as a Senior Associate with a company in London called Korn Ferry. Today's 'gold standard' is to address the particular needs and challenges of my clients.

I may no longer refer to myself as an athlete, but the skills, ambition and sheer desire to succeed will never abate.

CLOSING

At the end of the day everybody retires at some stage.

For many it's the end of something great but perhaps it's also the start of something great. It's a life where you can look back on your career and think about your greatest days and most memorable moments and ask did I actually do that and how did I do it?

Gordon D'Arcy was a brilliant rugby player. Today is works for the hugely successful banking and asset management group – Investec. Henry Shefflin won a record 10 All Ireland senior hurling medals. He works for one of Ireland's biggest banks – Bank Of Ireland and is one of RTE's top GAA pundits. Eoin Reddan enjoyed a hugely successful career in professional rugby both at home and abroad. He now works for Avolon – one of the biggest aircraft leasing companies in Europe. Derval O'Rourke is a former World sprint hurdles champion. She has a start-up business focusing on health and fitness.

The very best in sport struggle with retirement but there is life after sport. It's just a new life. A life off the stage. A life without training, travelling and competing. A life full of possibilities.

Let the second half begin.

A huge thank you to everybody who helped me with this book. I am incredibly grateful.

A very special thank you to all the people I interviewed. Thanks for trusting me to write your story. Thanks for saying yes.

To Dave Sheeran and Opel, a massive thank you for believing in this project and supporting it. Thanks also to Gillian Whittall.

Thank you to Frank, Andrew, Elaine, Shelley, Mairead and all at Lettertec Ireland.

Ray McManus you are a genius in the world of photography. Thanks for all your help with this book. A big thank you to Brendan Moran too.

In conclusion, I'd like to remember my friend Malachi Murray, who sadly passed away in 2015. He loved sport and is sadly missed. I'd also like to remember Tony Keady, a Galway hurling legend who died suddenly in August 2017.

Finally, I'd like to thank my best friends [you know who you are] and my family for all their love and support. My mother Theresa, sister Mary and brothers Frank and Derek. Thanks also to Laura, Sophie, Elaine, my godson Harry, Marian and Austin.

And thank you to my wonderful godparents Gabriel and Maureen Murphy.

Thank you for reading my book,

Paul

ABOUT THE AUTHOR

Paul Byrnes is an Executive Editor with RTÉ Television Sport. He was the Series Editor of The Sunday Game from 2004 to 2016.

He's also been Editor of RTÉ's Rugby coverage and has worked on many of the World's biggest sporting events. He was Acting Deputy Head of Television Sport in 2013.

He's worked on The Late Late Show and numerous other programmes in RTÉ. He was on the team that won an IFTA in 2004 for best sports documentary 'Final Words.'

Paul is from Oranmore in County Galway and this is his first book.

Paul.Byrnes@rte.ie